THE SWIMMING POOL

THE SWIMMING POOL

~

EVERYTHING
YOU NEED
TO KNOW
TO DESIGN,
BUILD, AND
LANDSCAPE
THE PERFECT
POOL
~

·TOM GRIFFITHS·

SIMON & SCHUSTER

SIMON & SCHUSTER
Rockefeller Center
1230 Avenue of the Americas
New York, New York 10020

SIMON & SCHUSTER and colophon are registered trademarks
of Simon & Schuster Inc.

A FRIEDMAN GROUP BOOK

©2001, 1994 Michael Friedman Publishing Group, Inc.

THE SWIMMING POOL
Everything You Need to Know to Design, Build, and Landscape the Perfect Pool
was prepared and produced by
Michael Friedman Publishing Group, Inc.
230 Fifth Avenue
New York, New York 10010

Editor: Elizabeth Viscott Sullivan
Art Director: Jeff Batzli
Designer: Kevin Ullrich
Photography Editor: Emilya Naymark

7 9 10 8 6

Library of Congress Cataloging-in-Publication Data
Griffiths, Tom
    The swimming pool: everything you need to know to design,
build, and landscape the perfect pool/by Tom Griffiths.
        p.   cm.
    Includes bibliographical reference and index.
    ISBN 0-671-88292-9 : $27.50
    1. Swimming pools.   2. Hot tubs.
TH4763.G75 1995
690'.89--dc20   94-13683
                                                         CIP

Color separations by United South Sea Graphic Art Co., Ltd.
Printed in China by Leefung-Asco Printers Ltd.

To my parents, for providing me with the Murray's Laurel Lake experience, and particularly to my brothers and my sister, Wally, Ray, and Monica, for sharing it with me.

To Roni, Kendra, and Rachel, my "seashell girls," for loving the water and my career as much as I do.

ACKNOWLEDGMENTS

For all of their help and support on this project, I would like to thank:

Steve Shinholser, American Pool Service;
Bob Steel, Dana Point, California;
Don Steel, University of Maryland;
Carvin DiGiovanni and Dave Karmol, National Spa
    & Pool Institute;
Perry Morgan, Penn State University;
Elizabeth Sullivan, Michael Friedman Publishing Group, Inc;
Neal Schwartz, pool builder;
Kai Eng, Eng Marketing, Inc;
Randy Smith, Clearwater Pools; and
Dave Griffith and Gail Armstrong, Penn State University.

CONTENTS

∎ ∎ ∎

Introduction

At age twelve, I took a summer job that would chart the course for my career. I worked as a paperboy for twenty-five cents an hour at Murray's Laurel Lake in Montvale, New Jersey. Actually, I wasn't a paperboy in the standard sense, but rather more of a "beachboy." I picked up discarded papers and other litter on the beach surrounding Frank Murray's "for-members-only" lake, where I later became a lifeguard. My two brothers, my sister, and I spent all our summers at Laurel Lake, and it was there that I gained a keen appreciation of swimming, aquatic sports, and water safety. In fact, my experience at Laurel Lake shaped my career. I teach water sports, currently manage five large swimming pools, and have written and lectured extensively on various aquatics topics.

The Swimming Pool is based upon the knowledge I have gained during my thirty-plus years of swimming pool experience and water-safety work. This book is intended to offer ideas and advice, from selecting a pool site and type to troubleshooting and maintenance. Above all, it is meant to help both novice and experienced pool owners keep their pools cleaner, safer, more enjoyable, and trouble-free.

■ ■ ■

POOLS PAST AND PRESENT

Although often believed to be a twentieth-century phenomenon, swimming pools date back more than five thousand years. Ancient pools resembled bathtubs and sinks, as they were simply filled with fresh water, then emptied when they became dirty. Filtration and circulation were not components of these pools.

The first pools, supposedly built for religious ceremonies, were found in India; within the remains of a building in Mohenjo-daro, archaeologists uncovered a pool that was 10 feet (3m) deep, 40 feet (12.2m) wide, and 60 feet (18.3m) long. This pool, larger than most of today's backyard pools, was constructed of hand-cut blocks of stone that were placed carefully to create a watertight shell, a feat that would be difficult to repeat even today.

Almost twenty-five hundred years ago, the Greeks built pools in both schools and homes. School pools were built specifically for physical training, whereas home pools were built by the wealthy primarily for entertainment and relaxation.

One of the oldest references to public swimming comes from Rome. As early as 215 B.C., *piscinae publicae* ("public fish ponds") were built specifically for swimming and exercise. Grandiose public baths were built for the emperors Nero, Titus, Caracalla, and Diocletian. By the height of the Roman Empire, public baths had grown in popularity, and many citizens spent much time exercising and relaxing at beautiful swimming facilities. Many ancient baths provided what would be considered modern amenities—tile finishes; heated, circulated water; and splendid changing rooms. Roman baths often offered hot, warm, and cold water.

The Romans also built baths in North Africa, England, France, and Germany, and as the popularity of the baths increased, privacy decreased. Wealthier citizens began to build their own pools to ensure privacy, just as homeowners do today.

With the fall of the Roman Empire came the decline of the swimming pool. In fact, public and private bathing did not

become popular again until the 1700s, when floating docks were placed in European rivers to facilitate swimming. It was not until the mid-1880s in England that swimming pools were built again with any regularity. Pool construction in England was probably inspired by the swimming pools that had been discovered in India.

At the beginning of the twentieth century, Adolph Sutro constructed one of America's most famous pools. Sutro's lifelong endorsement of swimming most likely came from his hometown of

Above: Detail from the tomb of Tuffatore, 490 B.C., The National Museum, Paestum, Greece. Below: Detail of a female athlete, third century A.D., Villa Casale, Piazza Armerina, Sicily.

Aachen, Germany, noted for its hot sulfur baths. Sutro built what is now known as the Sutro Baths, seven pools overlooking San Francisco Bay. The largest pool, laid out in an L-shaped design, measured 300 feet (91.4m) at its longest point and 175 feet (52.3m) at its widest. Five of these saltwater pools were aligned in a single row and heated to progressively higher temperatures; many of the heated pools were reserved for women and children. The pools were named according to their water temperatures: the large, unheated pool was known as the Freezing Pool, the warmest the Soup Bowl. The Sutro Baths contained more than five hundred private locker rooms, restaurants on three levels, seating for fifty-three hundred spectators, and many attractions that are contained only in today's water parks. But today, only ruins remain. The Sutro Baths closed shortly after World War II because of financial difficulties, and a mysterious fire finished them off in 1966. Although the Sutro Baths no longer function as pools, they still remain a major tourist attraction.

By the 1920s, swimming pools began to appear more regularly throughout the world, but were considered to be playthings of the rich and famous. Following World War II and the Korean War, swimming pool construction saw tremendous growth. Some claim this was because millions of people were given swimming training during these wars, which resulted in an interest in the sport, especially because it was coupled with major economic improvement in many countries in the postwar years. By 1970, there were more than a million pools in the United States alone, the majority of which were private backyard pools. Today the United States boasts nearly ten million pools: three million in-ground, just under three million above-ground, and approximately three million spas and hot tubs. France has about a half million, South Africa a quarter million, and Canada just under a million pools.

Today's swimming pools offer numerous benefits. A backyard pool provides a special place to spend time with family, neighbors, and friends. A pool provides a vacation spot in the summer, even year-round.

The primary reasons that homeowners invest in pools are that they want to beat the heat, increase physical fitness, and engage in family activities without using the car. Homeowners also want to swim and play in clean, bacteria-free water. Installing a pool can also increase the value and beauty of a home.

Pools are now within reach of most family budgets (see chapter four for more details), thanks to improved design and research by the swimming pool industry. But the purchase of a pool must be well planned. A well-planned pool is customized to blend in with one's home, yard, and lifestyle, and addresses the specific needs of children and adults.

The Neptune Pool at Hearst Castle, the former home of newspaper tycoon William Randolph Hearst. A Greco-Roman style pool, it had seventeen dressing rooms to accommodate Hearst's usual number of forty to fifty weekend guests, mainly Hollywood celebrities.

This free-form lake pool is a prime example of how a well-planned, naturalistic pool project can enhance a landscape. Notable features include lush vegetation, a stone border on the far side of the pool that contains a waterfall that cascades into the pool, and a wooden gazebo with a bar, a bridge, a pathway, and steps that link the pool patio area to the house.

Before building a new pool or renovating an old one, it is essential to observe the following steps. First, compile a list of pool builders and dealers in your area. A minimum of six residential swimming pools should actually be inspected, and it is best to check with some previous customers who have pools that are at least five years old. Don't be afraid to interview numerous pool professionals before narrowing the field to between three and five builders. Once you've chosen the finalists, request bids from each. Before signing a contract, consult consumer organizations, such as your local Better Business Bureau or chamber of commerce, to be sure that your prospective builder is licensed, insured, and follows the pool standards estab-

lished in your area. You should also obtain warranties for the pool and any equipment you buy.

Finally, it's vital to remember that a beautiful, clear swimming pool is not a magical occurrence, although to many a swimming pool appears to be a simple thing—a calm, still body of water, much like a full sink or bathtub. This resemblance is the only similarity. Both tubs and sinks are emptied quickly when their waters become dirty, but an effective swimming pool system does not allow its water to become dirty. In reality, a swimming pool is a dynamic system through which water continually flows to be cleaned, heated, and sanitized several times each day. Because of this sophisticated process, swimming pool water is often cleaner than the household water that is used to fill it. Put simply, maintaining a clean, clear pool does take time and effort.

Today's pools require filtered and chemically disinfected water. Without proper filtration and disinfection, pool water quickly turns cloudy and becomes filled with algae and bacteria, rendering the pool unattractive and unsafe. Conversely, a properly planned pool is a source of pride that is beautiful to behold and adds much to the quality of one's life. The five basic swimming pool circulation components are the pool pump, hair and lint strainer, filter, chemical feeder, and various inlets and outlets. To operate a safe and clean pool, every homeowner must have an understanding of these components. In fact, there are many other important elements in keeping a swimming pool safe and enjoyable—all of which will be discussed in the following chapters.

■ ■ ■

The Swimming Pool is divided into two sections. The first four chapters clearly detail how to install an affordable and functional pool on your lot and how to make it an attractive part of your landscape. These chapters are meant to give you an understanding of site development and construction, specific available pool types, and hot tubs and spas, as well as offer individual case studies that describe in detail a range of pools, from the very basic to the elaborate. The remaining chapters provide everything you need to know to maintain the pool properly, and they offer advice on equipment, safety, and barriers. Finally, it is my hope that this book will encourage you to invest in a swimming pool. I'm convinced that once you install one, you'll wonder why you waited so long.

As shown, attractive masonry can be installed to unite certain elements—in this case, waterfall, spa, and spillway—of the poolscape. Here, the surrounding vegetation gains presence thanks to the stone outcroppings of the waterfall.

Strong lines define this modern lap/reflecting pool. The contemporary architecture of the house and the sleek pool complement each other, and the landscaping of the entire property is well balanced.

Part I
PLANNING THE POOL

Chapter One

The Site

THERE ARE MANY FACTORS TO CONSIDER BEFORE INSTALLING A pool. Although developing the pool site is a comprehensive task, there's no need to feel intimidated by it: many professionals are available to assist you in the process. The principles set out in this chapter are meant to help you to understand and overcome common obstacles, although professional guidance will be necessary as well.

PROPER POOL PLACEMENT

The major pool-site considerations are as follows: legal restrictions; subsoil conditions and obstructions; sun, shade, and wind exposure; access to the pool and pool area; and views of and from the pool.

Dealing with Restrictions and Obstructions
Regardless of its size, shape, or slope, just about any yard can be fitted with a beautiful swimming pool. But successfully integrating the pool with the architecture

Natural stone outcroppings and lush landscaping provide the perfect setting for this naturalistic pool. The spacious deck made of brick pavers coordinates well with the pool and provides plenty of room for entertaining. The pool house adjacent to the raised spa adds function and visual balance.

of your home and landscape is extremely important and can be difficult to do.

First and foremost, you must be aware of any land-use restrictions that might apply to your property. Before even thinking of building a pool, study the zoning laws, deed restrictions, and building codes of your area. This way you will know the allowable size, type, and location of a pool for your property. Zoning laws, for example, often dictate front, side, and rear-yard setbacks, that is, how much space must remain between property lines and other buildings. There are often laws that determine how much of a yard may be covered with an impervious surface or structure. Height restrictions for fences and buildings are other considerations. Some home-owners' associations also mandate that utility easements are not interfered with. Your local government should have this information.

Do yourself a favor and take the following first step: take a look at a minimum of six other pool sites in your town or city. This is an enjoyable exercise and you'll learn a lot, especially if you take the time to converse with other pool owners. Find out about the land restrictions and zoning ordinances that affected their sites, then follow up by getting these regulations in writing from your local government. Although neighbors or friends can supply you with advice, never rely on this information regarding such matters as if it really were the law.

If you intend to install a permanent pool structure, you'll need a building permit before construction begins, and once it does, you'll need to be certain that all building codes are followed strictly. There may also be other local municipal restrictions and regulations that govern swimming pools. The use of water for filling pools and the discharging of that water, for example, may be severely restricted in your area. You may also need written approval of your fencing, pool cover, and pool type from your local government. Not until you clearly understand all applicable restrictive and regulatory guidelines for pools in your area can you seriously consider placing one in your yard.

Secondly, make every attempt to discover subsoil conditions and any obstructions in your yard before attempting to place your pool in the ground. Changing the size, shape, or layout of a pool after excavation begins is both time-consuming and expensive. If at all possible, drill test bores into the ground to help determine the condition of the soil. Rock, clay, a high water table, and other subsoil conditions can cause major excavation problems. Many pool builders include a subsoil clause in their contracts that explains additional costs that may be incurred should excavation efforts be hindered by rock, water, or unstable soil.

Other underground obstructions include septic tanks, dry-well systems, and plumbing. Overhead obstructions include overhead power lines that could fall into your pool or onto your deck. All structures—including storage sheds, garages, fences, walls, and the house itself—should be a minimum of 15 feet (4.6m) away from the pool's edge. If not, these structures can become inviting diving platforms for trespassers. If all these factors are considered prior to excavation, you'll save considerable time and money. Remember, it's far easier to move a pool on paper than it is to move it once excavation has begun. Moving a pool even a few feet in one direction can avoid many obstructions.

When excavation takes place, a large back hoe, loader, bobcat, and dump truck may be used to avoid the unnecessary handling of dirt. This heavy construction equipment needs a

Poolside boulders are an interesting accent in this free-form pool and spa combination. Slate was a good choice for the deck, as it provides a natural transition from the boulders to the pool.

way to gain access to the backyard safely and easily: a cartway of 8 to 10 feet (2.4 to 3m) wide is needed to move heavy equipment in and out of a yard. If less than an 8-foot width is available, earth removal with shovels and wheelbarrows may be required, resulting in a lengthy and expensive excavation project. Construction access may even have to come through a neighbor's yard. Earth disturbance can be surprising and scary, as a major construction job will look like a war zone before it is finished. Make sure to discuss the amount of earth disturbance with your pool builder early on, so you won't be surprised, financially or visually.

Soil conditions can also potentially damage a pool shell. Loam, sandy soil, wet soil, expansive soil, rock, and filled ground have special concerns associated with them, all of which should be fully analyzed by the builder.

If you have a flat lot, you can recycle the earth removed from the pool site to create mounds. Elevated mounds are a common technique that can provide privacy and creative landscaping of waterfalls or ornamental plantings. Earth mounding can do wonders for a flat lot by adding variety via customized slopes and hills, and at the same time, it can save money in removal costs.

Pools constructed on hillside lots are especially challenging projects, requiring expert advice. The cost of building a pool on a steep lot can be tremendous, but the rewards can also be great. Pools on hillside lots render once unusable land usable. In addition, the views from these pools can be spectacular. Steep-lot pools are often built on stilts, and many creative pool builders utilize slopes above these pools to create waterfalls. So if your home is on a hillside lot, you really needn't be discouraged from investigating the possibilities of installing a pool.

Another vital consideration in choosing the proper site for a pool is the location of existing utilities. A few calls to your local utility companies will take much of the guesswork out of this process. Utility company employees can quickly mark all underground lines and cables and explain appropriate setbacks to you for both above- and underground wires and cables.

A waterfall is more than an attractive visual addition to a poolscape. The sound of flowing water is soothing and looks perfectly natural in the profusely landscaped setting shown here.

Furthermore, every pool site requires the accessibility of these utilities: water, electricity, sewer or other acceptable drainage, and fuel for the heater (gas, propane, oil).

Along those lines, many naturalistic pool designs can "hide" filtration equipment in caves, alcoves, and shrubs. The filter and pump should be placed on a concrete slab that is specifically poured for the site. Precast concrete slabs are not recommended because as the ground settles, the slab may shift and damage the pool plumbing. The poured slab should be large enough to add equipment, like a pool heater, in the future.

Although weatherproof enclosures were once recommended for pool equipment, today's equipment can withstand just about any type of weather. Regardless of where the pool equipment is placed, there must be sufficient room to backwash and make repairs. For optimum performance, the filter and pump should not be located more than 50 feet (15.2m) away from the pool. If the pool pump is placed 2 feet (0.6m) higher than the pool grade, pump priming problems could result, making it difficult to maintain circulation. And don't hide pool recirculation equipment in your basement; the basement is an inconvenient location, and the equipment is loud and may cause flooding should it malfunction.

As just explained, there are many factors to consider regarding swimming pool placement and construction. But if you review and discuss these considerations with prospective pool builders, other pool owners, and your family, you will be better informed and will likely have eliminated any obstacles to installing a safe, enjoyable, and long-lasting pool.

Sun, Shade, and Wind

When attempting to place a pool properly on a lot, the elements of sun, shade, and wind must be considered to keep the water warm and swimmers comfortable in and around the pool.

The location of the swimming pool in relation to the sun is of paramount importance. Although direct sunlight on the pool is vital, the sunlight must not impair the view of the pool. In other words, the pool with its decking must be laid out so that the supervision of pool activities can be accomplished easily, and that means without excessive glare. In addition, extended sunlight throughout the day will not only keep swimmers more comfortable but will also decrease heating costs significantly. Except for pools that are built in desert or tropical climates where midday shade might be desirable, most pools are designed to maximize the sun and minimize the shade. As a rule, pools with southern and western exposures stay warmer than pools with northern and eastern exposures. Pools with dark bottoms absorb heat, keeping the water warmer, while pools with white bottoms reflect heat, keeping the water cooler.

While much attention should be given to sun exposure when positioning the pool, shady areas must be considered as well. Shade from trees and the house can offer a cool reprieve

Proximity of pool and house was a key consideration in this project, as the raised patio overlooking the pool links the swimming area to the house. Elaborate masonry, tile work, and shrubbery enhance the pool environment.

from the sun on hot days. Shade is an important consideration for adults as well, particularly grandparents or nannies who want to supervise children but must stay out of the sun. However, large trees that provide ample shade will also provide litter, dropping pods, blossoms, berries, and leaves into the pool, creating a poolkeeping nightmare. If shade is a priority for your pool surroundings, you may wish to obtain it by installing awnings, umbrellas, and similar structures located above and away from the pool deck. An overhead wooden trellis or gazebo can be strategically placed to provide shade and can also serve as a center for other recreational activities and for the supervision of the pool. Shade can also be produced by

Sometimes opposites attract. This tall, contemporary home seems to tower over the pool, providing a bird's-eye view of the water from the house. Nonetheless, both the house and pool are minimalistic. The straight lines and angular corners of the house are softened by the subtle, circular curves of the free-form pool, which adds visual interest and balance to the landscape.

installing an entire system of decks and trellises used to connect the house, backyard, and pool. But if you're going to manufacture shady areas in the yard, place them above the pool level to create a bird's-eye view of the pool for safety, supervision, and aesthetics.

Many naturalistic pools, particularly those that are designed to look like mountain lakes, do very well on shady lots. A little bit of debris on the surface only makes the pool look more natural, and extra cleaning equipment can be purchased to automatically clean the pool whenever it is not in use. (I prefer meticulously clean pools, without a trace of dirt or algae. My naturalistic pool would have a wider deck to keep debris away from the water.) A pool placed in the shade will have colder water than one placed in the sun. Moreover, swimmers may become cold when swimming or lounging in a shady pool environment. If a pool is to be placed in the shade, it's a good idea to turn up the pool heater a few degrees or even place heating coils in the pool deck.

In addition to sun and shade, wind is another important consideration. Blocking strong winds from blowing across the pool and its decking is just about as important as placing the pool in sunlight. A gentle breeze can have a positive cooling effect on loungers around the pool, but strong winds tend to be detrimental to the pool and bothersome for guests. Decreasing wind velocity is important because it keeps swimmers warmer and eliminates much of the evaporation and cooling of pool water, thereby saving you money. When swimming pool water evaporates, more than just water is lost; chemicals and heating costs are lost, too. Whenever possible, then, windbreaks should be placed on the perimeter of the property, particularly in the area from which the wind is traveling. Windbreaks can

be achieved with plants, trees, fencing, screens, walls, and other structures.

Access   A pool must be easily accessible from your house. Otherwise, much of the pleasure derived from using the pool will be overshadowed by the nuisance of getting to and from it. Changing facilities, whether in your home or in a bathhouse, should be conveniently linked to the pool by decks or walkways. Whenever possible, avoid constructing steps and other barriers to the pool; ramps are a better alternative, and are becoming a popular way of joining pool areas on different levels. Ample ramps and rails, along with some small steps, make entry easier for children and older adults. If small children are going to use the pool, be sure the shallow end is installed closest to where they will enter it, that is, closest to the exit from your home or bathhouse.

Generous poolside space should make it easy to get in and out of the pool and allow for activities like reading or sunbathing. It is also a good idea to create a space that will allow for as many activities as possible near the pool, including cooking and entertaining, so that trips back and forth to the house are minimal. Access to the pool should be such that swimmers are prevented from traveling across grass or dirt prior to entering the pool; otherwise, debris will enter the pool with each swimmer. If the access to your pool area and to the pool itself is not properly planned with these recommendations in mind, driving to a public pool might be a more convenient and far less expensive option.

Views   Generally speaking, the pool should be in complete view of the house yet laid out in harmony with it. The

This pool was designed with the view beyond in mind. A raised spa leads the eye to the increasing topography that culminates with the mountains in the distance. The fence serves many functions: it provides security, privacy, a windbreak, and a backdrop for plantings.

size of a pool should also be proportionate to the size and scale of a home. Several pictures of your existing home and yard should be analyzed to determine if the pool should be placed parallel, perpendicular, or at another angle to the house. You and the builder should jointly decide the angle at which the pool should be placed.

After evaluating all of the previously discussed logistics, it's time to select the exact location of the pool. This decision

can only be reached after considering aesthetics, safety, and privacy. Many creative pool designers believe that aesthetics is the key factor in deciding location, particularly when building naturalistic pools and waterscapes. Some designers claim that if sun, shade, wind, and other factors are too heavily considered, the pool will not be as attractive in the yard. So if a pool that is aesthetically pleasing is a priority, don't let drawbacks like leaves hamper your creativity. It's also a good idea to try to

highlight views both of and from the pool. The pool and decks should be oriented so that they can enhance the surrounding landscape. Vanishing-edge pools, for example, are tremendously popular because the view of these pools highlights vistas beyond them.

If small children will be using your pool, an unobstructed view from the house and yard is not only essential for safety reasons, but comforting to parents and other family members. You might want to consider placing adult amenities, such as spas and gazebos, so that they overlook the pool; this will not only create additional space for poolside activities, but produce a panoramic pool view that will help improve supervision enormously.

If privacy is a prime concern, don't place the pool in such a way that your neighbors have an excellent view of it. When telescopes begin to appear in neighboring homes shortly after the completion of your pool, you know it's time to invest in additional screening. (See pages 33–35 in this chapter for landscaping tips regarding privacy and chapter six for details on installing proper barriers.)

This vanishing-edge pool successfully creates the illusion that the pool water and the ocean beyond it are one. The large urn demonstrates how one single adornment can add a creative—and in this case, classical—touch to the poolscape. The raised spa offers a lovely view of the pool and sea.

■ ■ ■

DESIGNING THE LANDSCAPE

Although you can contract with landscape architects and pool builders to do all or part of your landscaping, it is important to be familiar with some landscape principles so that you are able to make wise decisions. Remember, you are decorating your pool much in the way you would decorate your house. Just as you would examine magazines and visit showrooms and model homes to get design ideas for the inside of your home, so should you do the same for this major outdoor project. Too often, the beauty of a pool is compromised by an unattractive or inadequate landscaping scheme.

Landscaping Objectives and Principles

Landscaping projects require thought and planning. Pool landscaping efforts must be customized to fit your pool, the ways in which you plan to use your pool, and your ability to maintain the pool area. Of course, all this must be thought of in terms of your budget.

First and foremost, make sure that the landscaping really works for your yard. Copying a neighbor's pretty landscape design may seem a good idea, but it may in fact create problems for you. It is important to realize that improper or poorly planned landscaping can hinder pool operation by blocking views, obstructing access, and littering the pool and deck with droppings. A good landscaping scheme serves many functions and is far more complex than installing plants. Pool fencing, decks, walkways, and poolside structures must be planned to complement one another as well as blend in with the house and yard.

Before you begin to landscape your pool area, decide on your landscaping needs. Beautification, privacy, safety, comfort, enjoyment, and convenience are a few of the more important pool landscaping considerations. For example, if keeping unwanted visitors out of the pool is a major concern, strong fencing with thorny bushes or vines may be preferred to a low-perimeter hedge. On the other hand, if space for entertaining is a priority, a spacious flat deck would be better than a profusion of plants and rock outcrops. If simple upkeep is a primary concern, that will influence your choice of plants and trees; you may even wish to keep planting to a minimum.

When selecting landscaping materials, you should bear in mind your lifestyle and work schedule. Retired homeowners may have a lot more time available to care for the landscape

This sunken-tile pool with Gothic windows overgrown with vines is a private, romantic hideaway seemingly from days gone by, thanks to the well-planned landscaping. Planters provide a touch of color, and the waterfall in the far corner enhances the poolscape's aesthetics.

than do younger couples with children. Some landscaping requires a great deal of care, such as flowering plants and shrubs that require fertilizing and trimming, or nonrustproof deck furniture that requires painting, so it is best to invest in attractive items that require little maintenance.

Price is an important consideration when you draw up your landscaping considerations. If your budget is limited, you may have to select only those landscape items that make your pool usable, and wait to buy the items on your "wish" list. For example, if you need trees or shrubs to screen your pool for privacy, these plantings probably would be high on your list of first buys. If beautification is a priority, then flowering annuals may be your first purchase. Rank your needs, then select

essential items that are within your budget. More expensive and lower-priority needs can always be added later—that's the nice thing about landscaping.

If you're on a limited budget, get the biggest bang for your buck by clustering your plants. Generally speaking, the larger the plant material, the more it's going to cost, so if you know you want some tall evergreens but can only afford three, place them close together rather than spreading them out. If you like flower beds but can't afford too many plants, make a small flower bed and buy fast-growing plants. As these plants grow, you can easily expand your bed. If you have a large bed with few plants in it, your plants will appear lost. For those with large landscaping budgets, I would recommend large trees for privacy at the perimeter of the lot, with smaller, exotic trees closer to the pool. A gazebo with plenty of deck space and walkways is a terrific addition, too.

The following six principles of landscaping should help you get started on a general landscaping plan. Bearing these principles in mind, you can move on to more specific landscaping ideas, some of which are included later in this chapter.

Order and Unity

Order is the overall organization and structure of a landscaping design. Unity is the harmonious relationship between all elements and characteristics of a design. To establish order, you must create a theme around your pool that is carried throughout your entire landscaping composition. To establish unity, you must fit all the pieces of the puzzle together so that they relate to one another. Without

A Hollywood producer wanted a dramatic poolscape and attained it by placing a circular pool in the middle of an enclosed garden. Fountains converging at the center of the pool add an elegant focal point that evokes a feeling of nostalgic glamour.

order and unity, your backyard poolscape will seem chaotic and unorganized. Home and garden magazines can give you ideas for creating order and unity.

Balance

Balance is the equalization of visual weight from one area of the landscape composition to another. While there will usually be a dominant accent in a composition, there should not be an imbalance of weight. There are usually two types of balance, symmetrical and asymmetrical. Symmetrical balance is achieved by creating a mirror image from one side of the pool to the other. Asymmetrical balance is achieved by creating equal weight without repetition of forms on opposite sides of the pool.

Rhythm

Rhythm is created in a pool environment by the repetition of outstanding elements. If a dramatic effect is desired, you should emphasize the rhythmic aspects of a pool. If you want a visually relaxed atmosphere, you should reduce the rhythms. For example, to achieve a relaxed rhythmic pattern, you should choose plants that do not stand out visually.

Dominance

Dominance is the authority of one design element over all others, and is achieved by size, shape, tone, color, texture, or location. The subordination of other elements in the design establishes a certain unity among them, causing the unique element to become dominant. Dominant elements in the design are sometimes referred to as focal points. For example, a flowering tree, a large rock, or a waterfall can create a focal point, or dominance. In most poolscapes, the pool itself is the dominant landscape feature, based on sheer size alone.

This tranquil pool perfectly reflects the focal point on this attractive landscape, but it offers far more than aesthetics, as its shape is conducive to both lap and recreational swimming. Wide recessed steps on opposite sides of the pool make for easy access as well.

Contrast Closely related to dominance, contrast is the visual strength of one element or a group of elements that is different than the remainder, which helps provide interest and unity to a design. Contrast can often create a sense of tension in a design. A tall tree in a predominantly flat landscape, for example, serves as a strong visual contrast.

Interconnection Interconnection is a principle of design in which unity, balance, and order are achieved by physically linking various elements into one unified composition. In the pool area, interconnection can be achieved by a series of adjacent or overlapping elements, such as plants, fences, walls, walkways, pool decking, and patios. Attractive ground covers can also be valuable in developing interconnection in a landscaping design.

Site Inventory and Analysis
Keeping in mind the landscaping principles just discussed, the next step in planning your pool is to study the existing site by completing an inventory and analysis of the pool area. A site inventory means that you have to assess and evaluate the site conditions that will have a significant influence on your design. The inventory should include items such as the character of the site, local codes, drainage, type of soil or soils, views, vegetation, and microclimate. As you develop your pool-site plan, design it with the characteristics from the inventory in mind. Remember, the inventory is simply an accurate assessment of the current status of the site environment and any restrictions that you face in installing your pool.

The basis of a site analysis is provided by creating an accurate base map of the property on which are recorded all physical site elements such as walls, fences, and other miscellaneous buildings and structures. The property should be measured and boundaries defined using a tax map or other official record of the lot dimensions. Of particular concern are the front-, side-, and rear-yard setbacks; these indicate how close to each boundary the homeowner is allowed to build a structure. The setback lines are clearly drawn on all approved building lots. Your local city hall, county office, or mortgage banker may be able to supply helpful documents illustrating these elements of your property.

After boundaries and measurements are taken, the house should be drawn to scale on the base map. This drawing should indicate the location of all walls, doors, and windows as

This naturalistic pool is a perfect complement to the architecture of this home. Note how the outcroppings and patio lend to the "pool-in-the-middle-of-a-rock-garden" effect.

well as utilities such as gas, electric lines and outlets, television cables, dryer vents, and existing lighting. (To assist homeowners and contractors, many utility companies will print "Call us before you dig" on approved building lot plans and include a toll-free telephone number.) The house's architectural style should be noted along with the color and texture of its exterior. The base map need not be a work of art, but it should be as complete and accurate as possible.

The microclimate of the pool site needs to be analyzed, too. The times of sunrise and sunset should be noted for various times of the year so that sun and shade areas may be planned. The direction and velocity of prevailing winds, particularly summer breezes, must also be noted for the positioning of windbreaks.

At this point, the site should be photographed from several angles. The photographs will not only improve the accuracy of your drawing, but also provide a before-and-after look at your poolscape.

In addition to recording and observing what exists on your property, it is important to note the characteristics of your neighborhood. Take into consideration the style of the other homes as well as the size and maturity of neighborhood trees and plantings so that your landscaping efforts blend in naturally. Sidewalks, street lights, and neighborhood traffic patterns are also important, for knowing the direction of traffic and busy times of the day will help you determine if and where visual and noise screening should be installed.

Of utmost importance are the views to and from the pool. You may want to highlight some of these and obscure others, bearing in mind that these views will change over the seasons of the year. Mark these views, then consider storage areas,

Site Inventory and Analysis: The Base Map

Determining What Actually Exists

■ **Draw the actual dimensions of your lot:** use tax maps, plot plans, architectural drawings, and contour maps supplied by your local bank or municipality.

■ **Note the exact location of your house:** include the precise location of doors, windows, and entry and exit points for both the house and yard.

■ **Mark existing structures:** precisely place fences, walls, walkways, patios, decks, garages, storage sheds, and other structures on your map.

■ **List easements and right-of-ways:** look for these on your deed.

■ **Illustrate utility lines and other obstructions:** note overhead lines and cables and underground gas, sewer, water, electric, cable, and septic tanks. Utility companies can be most helpful here.

■ **Draw front-, side-, and rear-yard setbacks:** contact your zoning or code official for this information.

■ **Pinpoint electric outlets,** hose bibs, air-conditioning units, lighting fixtures, meter boxes, and so on: decide what you must see and access with ease and what you must hide.

■ **Mark notable landscaping features:** decide which trees, shrubs, and rocks you want to highlight or remove.

■ **Note views, both good and bad:** mark those views you want to enhance and those that need to be eliminated or reduced.

■ **Describe the microclimate:** accurately mark the points of the compass and the direction of the sun and the wind.

■ **Take several photographs of the site:** do this to improve accuracy of your base map and provide "before" and "after" assessments.

---

work stations, and service entries; these areas must be marked so that they can be somewhat hidden by strategic plantings but at the same time remain accessible and functional.

After you complete the base map of the specific features and elements that exist on the site, you can compose a functional diagram of the future site. The ideal functional diagram is a graphic development of your landscape design (see pages 34–35). It need not be a work of art, but should include a rough illustration of the major functional areas of the site, noting the distances between each area, the type of enclosure you want for each area, and any barriers or screens, exit and entry points, and views you would like to hide or highlight. It is important to define your usage areas, be they for recreation, relaxation, gardening, work storage, or service, and allow sufficient space for each. When dealing with different spaces within the poolscape, it might be helpful to identify each as public, semi-public, semiprivate, or private to facilitate selecting appropriate barriers, screens, and planting buffers. Circulation patterns

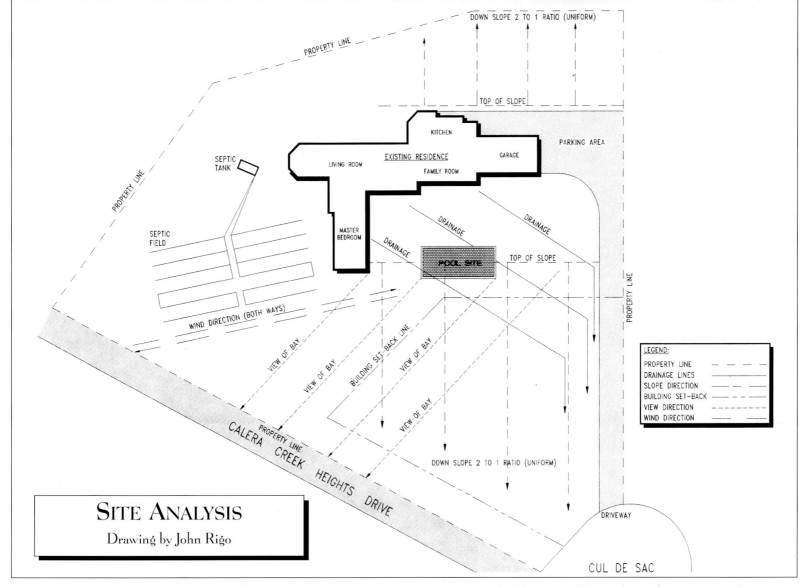

SITE ANALYSIS

Drawing by John Rigo

Site analysis is a significant step toward completing a successful pool project. This drawing and the checklist on the opposite page should help you identify the critical points of your prospective pool site.

must also be drawn so that heavy traffic is not channeled through private areas intended for relaxation.

Once you have completed your plans for your poolscape, you need to concentrate on selecting the appropriate ground covers, shrubs and trees, fencing and screens, decks and walkways, bridges or waterfalls, and lighting.

Plants by the Pool
Besides creating a beautiful natural setting for a pool, plants add texture and color to the

swimming environment. Landscape architects, landscapers, nursery workers, and regional horticultural guides can offer helpful advice regarding final planting decisions. (Specific suggestions for a range of plantings can be found in the chart in the appendix on page 136.)

Generally speaking, pool plants should be hardy, healthy, and sun-loving. They should like water and be mildew-resistant. When it comes to decorating with beautiful flowering plants, thousands of options are available, with annuals being

The Ideal Functional Diagram

Determining What Could Be

■ **Note the character of the neighborhood:** consider the style of the homes, traffic patterns, and sidewalks. How will your poolscape blend in?

■ **Clearly mark entries, exits, and passageways:** plot the ideal places for foot traffic to take place; clearly mark exit and entry points in the pool area. How will this traffic be channeled?

■ **Define usage areas:** carefully place recreation, relaxation, work, storage, entertainment, and service areas. How will you identify, enclose, and screen these areas?

■ **State security and privacy concerns:** secure the pool. What type of fencing is required? What type of landscaping will be used for buffers?

■ **Note views and vistas:** consider the views. Which views do you want to highlight? Which would you like to hide or screen?

■ **List preferred plantings:** prioritize your plantings. Which must you purchase first? Which can you delay purchasing?

---

the most popular. When selecting flowering plants, be certain they blossom during the summer months.

Special consideration should be given to plants and trees that do not attract annoying insects and that do not drop leaves excessively. Unfortunately, some of the prettiest plants and flowers can cause problems if they draw bees or shed a great deal. Remember, when it comes to pool plants, looks are not everything.

Raised Beds and Container Gardening   There are other important considerations in poolside planting. Greenery and flowering plants should be carefully placed so that water running off the deck will provide moisture for the plants. Conversely, runoff from the plants should not be deposited on the deck or in the pool. Properly placed borders of flagstones

or other landscaping materials can help to keep mulch and dirt off the deck and out of the pool.

Planting flowers in raised beds offers a great swimming-pool planting scheme. Raised beds serve several functions: they can add visual relief or contrast to a flat lot, add prominence to some special plantings, create separate and distinct clusters, and contain the soil so that it does not enter the pool. The borders of the beds can double as pool benches and retaining walls. In addition, raised beds elevate flowers and plants to a height that makes maintenance easier. Remember, when raised beds are constructed, they must be built with drainage in mind. Bottom drainage or weep holes must be supplied so that the draining water doesn't find its way into the pool.

Container plants do extremely well around swimming pools. Perhaps the greatest advantage of container plants is

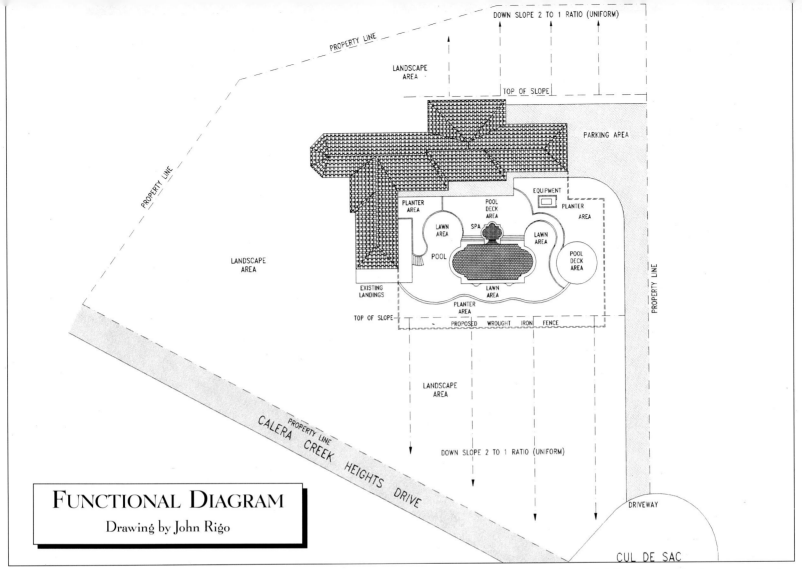

FUNCTIONAL DIAGRAM

Drawing by John Rigo

Following the site analysis, a functional diagram is the next step in planning your pool. This diagram helps you fine-tune the project, as it combines the pool, deck, lawn, fence, and sloped areas to complete the poolscape puzzle. The functional diagram should clearly indicate what the finished project will look like.

their portability. You can easily move potted plants to the pool for special occasions or move them when they drop flowers and leaves, attract bees, or take up needed space. Another advantage to container plants is that containers can be filled with the perfect soil, which is most convenient for sites where the soil is poor or unsuitable for pool plantings. Lightweight potting mixtures, which can be purchased from any nursery or garden shop, will provide good soil and will also lighten the load when you move the plants around the pool. However,

potted plants tend to dry out quickly, so they may need to be watered and fertilized more often.

Many types of containers can be used around the pool, as long as they are unbreakable. While clay, ceramic, and stone pots will certainly add to the aesthetic appeal of your pool, half-barrels, crates, and other plastic or wooden containers may be preferable in order to prevent accidents. Larger pots are also preferable, as they cannot be knocked over easily and can hold more water.

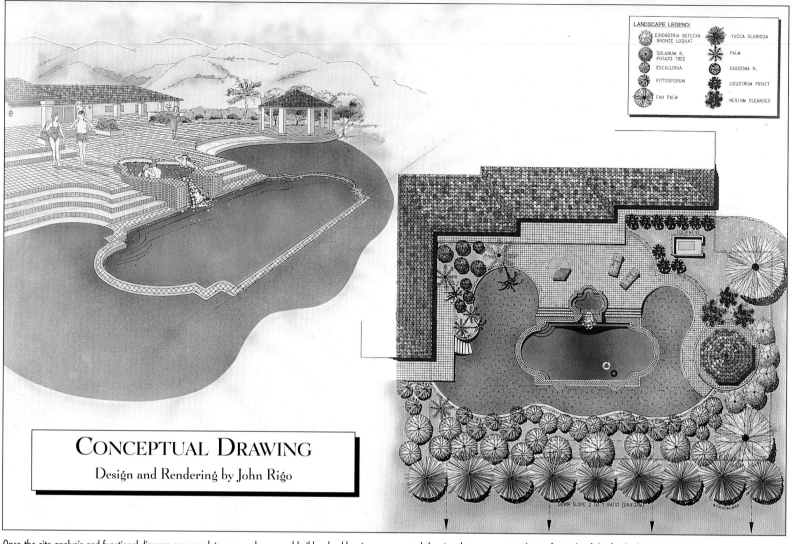

LANDSCAPE LEGEND:

ERIOBOTRIA DEFLEXA BRONZE LOQUAT		YUCCA GLORIOSA	
SOLANUM R. POTATO TREE		PALM	
ESCALLONIA		GARDENIA V.	
PITTOSPORUM		LIGUSTRUM PRIVET	
FAN PALM		NERIUM OLEANDER	

CONCEPTUAL DRAWING

Design and Rendering by John Rigo

Once the site analysis and functional diagram are complete, you and your pool builder should review a conceptual drawing that represents a decent facsimile of the finished project.

Ground Covers   The importance of a good ground cover around a pool or spa should not be overlooked. By definition, ground cover is any low or spreading plant that does not grow taller than 6 to 12 inches (15.2 to 30.5cm). There are a variety of flowering, nonflowering, woody, and herbaceous ground covers—and they possess almost as many functions. Around the pool, ground covers are useful in defining "nonwalking" areas, especially when used alongside paved walkways or lawns. Ground covers of distinct colors and textures can be used to create visual interest, while more neutral plants of this sort can also provide a noncompetitive background for more dominant landscaping elements like sculpture and ornamental trees. Ground covers may be used to interconnect other plants in the area. But perhaps most importantly, ground cover is an excellent way to cover areas where lawn and other plant materials are impractical. For instance, it can be dangerous and impractical to plant grass on steep slopes. In this situation, ground covers stabilize soils and prevent erosion. Ground covers can be planted where grass would be difficult to mow. Over the long haul, ground covers will save you time, effort, and money in landscaping maintenance. Check with your local nursery before buying ground covers to be certain whether the plants will prosper in the sun or shade of your pool area.

The finished project. This award-winning, traditional-style pool with raised spa cascading into the pool perfectly complements the architecture of the house. The spacious deck and steps invite the swimmer to enter the pool. All of the tiles in the project were individually cut—more than a year's work for the stonecutter.

Shrubs and Trees Shrubs come in various sizes and, based upon their size, serve different functions in a pool landscape. Low shrubs are woody plants that do not grow taller than 3 feet (0.9m). Similar to ground covers, they can be used to enclose areas as well as to define walks and patios. Low shrubs are a nice addition to the poolscape because they can be used to define these spaces without obstructing views. Intermediate shrubs are from 3 to 6 feet (0.9 to 1.8m) tall. They are used mostly to provide a transition in the landscape between low shrubs and trees. Tall shrubs are woody plants

from 6 to 10 feet (1.8 to 3m) tall, and are best used for vertical enclosures, screening for the elements, and privacy control.

Shrubs and trees that grow closely together form hedges. Hedges can be used to screen or hide pool equipment, camouflage other unattractive sites, and channel traffic. Hedges may be formal or informal. Formal hedges are made up of finely textured small-leaf plants, such as boxwood, that are manicured to a sharp straight edge and are found in many formal gardens. Formal hedges require careful attention and frequent trimmings. Informal hedges are usually composed of plants of a coarser texture, such as a large-leaf holly, which requires less care and provides excellent screening.

Effective visual screens, trees can be used to block wind and sun as well. Evergreen trees rather than deciduous trees are often selected for a poolscape because falling needles are usually less of a problem than leaves—although needles may drop all year long. Evergreen trees provide permanent, consistent screening and privacy, and proper evergreen plantings may reduce wind velocity by up to 60 percent. Coniferous evergreens, such as white pine, spruce, hemlock, yew, and juniper, maintain their color all year long without visible flowers. Evergreens are also available in shiny broadleaf varieties, such as rhododendron, mountain laurel, and leucothoe, adding luminescence to any outdoor space as well as offering the benefit of spectacular spring blooms.

Deciduous trees and flowering trees in a pool landscape may be used in order to contrast the light color of the blossoming flowers against the dark background of the evergreens. Deciduous trees can offer striking color changes within changing seasons, something to consider when your pool season is not year-round. Purple, red, yellow, and blue are just some of the brilliant colors that can be pleasingly combined. Fruit trees, such as hollies, oranges, and persimmons, can provide colorful flowers and fruit, but should be planted well away from the pool and deck area. Otherwise, their droppings will create a lot of cleanup work for you. You must also be cautious in planting trees near the pool, for their root systems may clog pipes or disrupt deck foundations and walkways.

Nonetheless, there are many small trees with good garden manners and root systems that are compatible with decks, patios, and walls. These trees don't shed many leaves, fruit, or blossoms. They are also slow to grow and, as a result, don't require a lot of pruning.

If your lot is large, a large shade tree or trees may be an effective backdrop for a naturalistic look. Flowering and majestic trees may be overwhelming on small lots and may shed too much for the meticulous pool owner. Nevertheless, large shade trees can often become the cool meeting place or picnic area in many yards.

There are also small trees available that have distinctive foliage. These trees are excellent for providing contrast to a landscape. The Japanese maple, *Acer palmature*, is a good example of a tree that can add variety to a pool landscape design. A small, slow-growing tree that does not grow taller than 15 feet (4.5m), the Japanese maple is hardy, with lacy foliage capable of bringing a bit of the forest into the smallest of poolscapes.

Remember, before purchasing any tree, pay critical attention to its eventual height and width (listed on its label). Otherwise, you may be asking for trouble.

Perimeter Fencing, Walls, Screens, and Other Structures

Constructing screens with fences and walls may be preferable to installing trees and shrubs, particularly since cleanliness is a top pool priority. Fencing on the perimeter of the lot provides security and privacy. Before constructing any fence, though, remember to check your local building codes and zoning ordinances.

Vertical screens are placed in pool-landscape designs to protect against unwanted sun, wind, noise, and unpleasant views. These screens can be used to define space and are typically lighter than fencing or walls, and are often less perma-

Who says a barrier has to be dull? The terra-cotta and Mexican in-laid tile murals shown here are functional and beautiful. The diagonal stripes on the pool bottom not only are visually compelling, providing a nice contrast to the wall, but also clearly define water depth.

nent so they cannot be considered safety barriers. Reed, wood lath, louvered wood, safety glass, plastic, canvas, and plants can be used as screens. Horizontal overhead structures can also be added to provide shelter from the sun; these can be made from a variety of materials such as wood, arbor and louvered overhead, tinted safety glass or acrylic, and sliding and stretched canvas awnings.

A variety of useful pool structures can be added to the landscape design as well. Gazebos have always been popular, for not only are they attractive, they provide additional space for entertaining, dining, changing clothing, storing items, and observing poolside activities. Similar to fencing, gazebos must blend in with the design of the house, pool, and yard. Many pool owners hide the back of a poolside gazebo with evergreens or vines to provide a more complete closure for privacy while keeping the side that faces the pool open for supervision. Other gazebos on the property should remain open to provide views of the pool and surrounding plantings.

Although the primary use of a bathhouse is to provide a place to shower and change, it can also be a place for storage and cooking. Bathhouses, then, can range from the simple to the elaborate. Some pool owners incorporate saunas into their bathhouses. Other structures that can be added to a pool landscaping design include a pool chemical shed, a greenhouse, a garden work center, or a garden pavilion.

Decks and Walkways

Pool decking and walkways that connect other functional yard areas are an integral part of every landscaping design. Decks provide extra space for poolside activities and transitional points for different areas around the pool. The importance of a quality pool deck is often overlooked by some homeowners. Don't make this mistake.

The deck is second in importance only to the swimming pool, and in some smaller yards, the deck may even take up all the space that is not devoted to the swimming pool; in most cases, the larger the deck, the better. All pool decks must be a minimum of 4 feet (1.2m) wide to allow safe pedestrian passage around the pool, should be clear and unobstructed at all times, and should extend at least 8 feet (2.4m) behind play equipment such as slides and diving boards. These are the minimum deck requirements.

A variety of materials is available for swimming pool decks. Provided the slope away from the pool is adequate and the material is completely nonslip, most materials can be used. Some of the more popular decking materials include pressure-treated wood, poured concrete, exposed aggregate concrete, slate, brick, ceramic tile, and flow-through interlocking tiles. It is important to select a deck that has heat-reflecting properties so that it is not too hot for bare feet. This type of material is referred to as cool deck. Carpeted decks are generally not suited for swimming pools because they retain moisture. To add variety to pool decks and walkways, decking materials such as brick and pressure-treated wood can be combined. If you use ceramic tiles or bricks for your pool deck, remember that it is the grout between the tiles and bricks that provides most of the abrasion that prevents slippage. Larger tiles and bricks are often slippery when wet, regardless of how nonslip the manufacturer claims them to be, for large tile and bricks allow bare feet to hydroplane across the surface. Basically, the smaller the tile or brick, the more nonslip the deck.

The deck must also slope away from the pool so that water that is splashed out of the pool—which picks up contaminants—is unable to return to the pool. The slope of the deck should be at least a quarter of an inch per foot (20.8mm/m) away from the pool or toward deck drains. The deck should be as close to the water surface as possible, as decks that are too far above the surface will make it difficult to enter and exit the pool and create more of a risk for divers. Ideally, decks should be 4 to 10 inches (10.2 to 25.4cm) above the water.

It is also wise to maximize deck space and minimize the lawn around your pool. As mentioned earlier, wet swimmers returning from the lawn to the pool bring grass and contaminants along with them; this is particularly true if the surrounding lawn has been recently cut. Lawns are pretty, but they create poolkeeping problems. If lawns are a must, separating pool (wet) and lawn (dry) activities with barriers such as fencing or planting is wise. This is why it is a good idea to install a large, spacious deck around the pool; doing so will increase the number of poolside activities that can occur simultaneously and prevent debris from entering the water.

Above: This poolscape incorporates trellises and vines to provide ample reprieve from the sun. The red-stained wood complements the red brick deck, and the randomly designed pool edge adds visual interest to what would be a long, narrow, unremarkable pool otherwise. Left: Not a straight edge can be found anywhere in this creative yet functional pool. Features of note are the wedding-cake steps at both ends of the pool, the in-water bench, and the raised spa.

White arbors and planters direct the eye toward this stately pool and spa. The entire project is united by spacious decking that assists in maintenance, as landscaping is kept on the periphery of the pool. The pool-house contains a large bar and grill, making this pool an ideal spot for entertaining.

When choosing natural stone for the pool deck, make sure the stone is colorfast. If it is not, it will leach into the pool and discolor the water and pool shell.

Coping, the material that provides a finishing edge to the pool, thus connecting the decking material to the pool wall, is also of vital importance, as it prevents water from finding its way behind the pool shell and is the place of entry for most swimmers. Coping stones must be sturdy, nonslip, and attractive. Tile, stone, concrete, and numerous other materials are available for coping. Many naturalistic pools use specially cut stones for this purpose. To eliminate a manufactured look of pool decking meeting the pool wall, try to place the coping over and beyond the wall (about 2 to 3 inches [5 to 7.5cm]) to create a lip.

While the same characteristics are required of materials used for walkways as for the pool deck, it is possible to use a

different surface for them as they won't receive quite as much exposure. For instance, wood rounds, concrete slabs, bricks in sand, gravel or crushed rock, and random stepping-stones make for excellent walkways but poor swimming pool decks, as they are not completely impervious to the elements.

When selecting natural stones for pool decks, coping, or walkways, or as accents, it is important to determine if the stone is colorfast; if not, the color can bleed or leach into the pool, discoloring the pool water and shell. Pennsylvania Blue flagstone is hard and colorfast, making an excellent coping stone for a naturalistic look, while Tennessee flagstone, although attractive, has a high iron content that may cause brown staining in the pool. These days, exposed aggregate concrete is being used more for decks and walkways, as it is extremely functional and attractive.

Bridges and Waterfalls

Bridges and waterfalls are becoming a more popular feature of pools today. Bridges offer a passageway from one area to another for both the swimmer and the dry observer, allow nonswimmers to experience the pool up close without getting wet, and enhance poolside entertaining. Most often, bridges over pools are constructed of wood or some combination of stone and concrete. The bridge must be sturdy, and children cannot be allowed to play unsupervised underneath it.

Waterfalls are a nice pool enhancement, providing more than aesthetics: they can be added on to the existing recirculation system so that an extra pump is not required. Many waterfalls are built with benches constructed directly underneath the fall of water, allowing children and adults to have fun and cool off at the same time. Waterfalls should be built

Swimming at night demands appropriate lighting. Today, there are many attractive options on the market that will make your pool safe and enhance its beauty. An underwater light (shown here at the far end of the pool) is of primary importance, as it allows swimmers and divers to determine water depth and makes proper supervision possible.

with variable speeds so that the intensity of water flow can be controlled by simply turning a valve. Those waterfalls that drop from a height greater than 4 feet (1.2m) should be shielded from the wind; otherwise decks and observers may inadvertently get wet on windy days. Waterfalls can also be designed as water slides. Water slides must have sufficient water depth (this will depend on who will be using it) where people come off them into the water. In the evening, a waterfall highlighted with either spotlights or colored accents is very pretty. If you opt for a waterfall, make sure the pool builder has experience constructing one, as not everyone can do this.

Lighting

Pool lighting has come a long way since the days when bright spotlights were mounted on garages to aim harsh beams on pool surfaces. Not only is spotlighting unappealing, it produces a dangerous glare on the surface of the water, which prevents one from being able to see under the water surface. Today's improved outdoor pool lighting can provide safety, security, and decoration. A variety of pool lighting is available that will enable you to illuminate your pool for evening swims and beautify it at night.

At least one underwater light is required for evening swimming. This way, swimmers and divers can determine water depth, and adequate supervision is made possible. This light is usually placed at the deep end of the pool, 3 to 4 feet (0.9 to 1.2m) below the surface; the larger the pool, the more underwater lights that are necessary. Underwater lights should point away from the house whenever possible so that there is no blinding glare.

The pool and pool area must also be illuminated from above the pool surface. Between 10 and 30 foot candles (110 to 330 LUX) as measured by a light meter are recommended for outdoor decks and pools, and must illuminate all walkways and decks to prevent injuries. The surface of the pool must be illuminated as well, but the light used there must not produce a glare. Most of this important down-lighting is provided by 120-volt outdoor lighting systems. This same lighting can also be used for highlighting elements of your landscape, such as a special tree, garden, or statues.

A variety of low-voltage lights can be placed in and around the pool for ambience. These can be installed by plugging in a small transformer and a two wired outdoor cable along the ground and adding fixtures wherever you need them.

Dramatic lighting can enhance many pool projects. Above: Here, lighting is used to showcase particularly attractive aspects of the pool landscaping. Left: Lighting is carefully placed to bring attention to the pool, home, and ornamental plantings, thus uniting and adding drama to the poolscape.

Low-voltage (12-volt) landscaping lights are ideal for this function and available in many varieties. Small landscaping spotlights can be purchased to illuminate special features such as waterfalls or grottoes. On straight-edge pools, low-voltage tube lighting can be placed around the perimeter of the pool to achieve a neon-light effect. Tiny bud lights can be used to define steps or decorate trees and shrubs. It must be remembered that ambience, not illumination, is the main function of 12-volt lighting.

There is much to consider when fitting a pool on your property. Remember, the more you do before beginning to install the pool, the more satisfying and trouble-free the job will be. If you follow the recommendations in this chapter, there should be no reason why your project should not result in a safe, enjoyable, clean, and beautiful pool.

Chapter Two

The Pool

ONCE THE POOL SITE HAS BEEN CHOSEN, IT'S TIME TO SELECT AND install the type, size, shape, and shell of your pool. Now the fun begins! Most people imagine the "traditional" swimming pool as being rectangular, but this standard pool is quickly becoming a thing of the past. The size and shape of your pool is completely up to you, although it is important to keep in mind that individual pool programming dictates pool dimensions.

FORM FOLLOWS FUNCTION

The average six-lane competition pool is approximately 45 × 75 feet (13.7 × 22.9m), or 3,375 square feet (313.9 sq m) of surface area. Obviously, few residential pools approach this size. A large residential swimming pool would be approximately 32 × 60 feet (9.8 × 18.3m), or 1,920 square feet (178.6 sq m) of surface area. If there is such a thing as an average-size swimming pool, it would probably cover 20 × 40 feet (6.1 × 12.2m), or 800 square feet (74.4 sq m), and hold approximately 25,000 gallons (95,000l) of water. Anything smaller would be considered a small pool.

This Lazy L—shaped pool seems to wrap around the house, its inventive lines a nice match for the contemporary architecture. The layout of the pool helps insure safety, as it keeps diving and swimming in separate areas of the water.

Most pools also range in depth from 3 1/2 feet (1.1m) in the shallow end to 5 feet (1.5m) in the deep end. But if diving is to be permitted, particularly from a springboard, the pool must have a lot of deep water. Every homeowner must address the issue of headfirst diving in the early stages of planning. Unfortunately, there is no universal agreement on what constitutes a safe diving depth. While some swimming pool organizations suggest as little as 7 1/2 feet (2.3m), some water safety experts suggest as much as 11 feet (3.4m). If diving is planned for the pool, I would suggest a minimum of 10 feet (3m). A safe diving area should have 10 feet of water under the tip of the diving board, and this depth must be extended at least 16 feet

(4.9m) out in front of and to the sides of the diving board, resulting in 1,300 square feet (121 sq m) of very deep water.

More important than the safe diving depth and distance is the supervision of those doing the diving. No diving dimensions can safely support show-offs, particularly adults, who are performing acrobatics from a diving board. If you are considering installing a diving board, you simply must have sufficient water depth, constantly supervise diving activities, and limit diving to children under twelve. In short, diving requires a lot of water for an activity that may only be enjoyed by a few.

As for diving from the side of the pool, this can be especially dangerous in less than 6 feet (1.8m) of water, so you might consider banning all headfirst entries from the pool deck in shallower areas. I cannot stress enough how important it is to keep these recommendations in mind.

Whether you opt for a concrete, vinyl-lined, or fiberglass pool, there are a few other basic points to bear in mind regarding water depth. Pools that are deeper than 5 feet (1.5m) are on the decline; in fact, 80 percent of the water in today's pools is less than 5 feet deep. Not only are construction costs higher for deeper pools, the costs associated with heating, filtering, and chemically treating the water increase in proportion to the volume of water in the pool as well. There are also greater safety risks with deeper pools, as nonswimmers can easily and suddenly get in over their heads. Rescues are more difficult in deeper water, too.

Also related to depth is the location of entry and exit points. If sufficient entry and exit points are not planned prop-

Clearly defined circular steps and a handrail not only make entering and exiting the pool safe and easy, they also point the way into the pool and spa.

erly, pool users will be constantly struggling to climb over the sides. Whenever possible, install ladders or steps at both the shallow and deep ends of the pool. Recessed steps are becoming more popular than ladders because of the safety and convenience advantages that steps offer. Zero-depth pools are also becoming popular. These are pools that offer a walk-in entry into the pool, which is great for toddlers, seniors, and disabled individuals, and can be used to enhance natural settings.

Concerning pool shapes, long, narrow pools tend to be more functional than shorter, wider pools. Long, narrow pools support more swimming and fitness activities and are often more pleasing to the eye than their shorter, wider counterparts. Although the choices for most above-ground pools and in-ground fiberglass pools are limited as far as size and shape, just about any form can be constructed for an in-ground concrete pool. Limitless pool shapes and contours can be accomplished by a creative pool builder and an imaginative homeowner. You can even construct a pool to reflect a special interest or hobby, just like celebrities do. (Can you guess the innovative pool shapes of Elvis Presley and Liberace?)

No matter what type of pool you build, changes in depth and in the bottom contour of the pool should be highlighted carefully for safety. It's surprising but true: people cannot determine water depth just by looking at a pool from the deck. Unbelievably, some pool contractors forget or ignore this vital detail. Depth should be marked horizontally on the pool deck and vertically on the pool wall whenever possible. The words "shallow" and "deep" should also be marked on opposite ends of the pool. Paint or tile of contrasting colors works best to illustrate changing depths. All depth markers should be a minimum of 4 inches (10.2cm) high, and should be located wherever there is a change in depth of 2 feet (0.6m). A safety line on the surface should also be used to prevent nonswimmers from slipping from shallow to deep water.

If you have decided on a naturalistic pool, you might feel that the safety markers are an aesthetic detraction. Your builder may be able to mark the pool effectively without ruining its natural look. And regardless of the theme or style of your pool, if lap swimming is important to you, a dark guide line on the bottom is a good idea.

■ ■ ■

ABOVE-GROUND POOLS

Most above-ground pools are round, although some are rectangular or oval. The above-ground pool can offer many advantages and benefits. No excavation is required because the above-ground pool simply lies on top of the ground and can be installed in a matter of days—even hours in some cases. This pool can be removed just as quickly—a big advantage if you plan on relocating soon. Above-ground pools are shallow water pools with a constant depth (usually 4 feet [1.2m]), so all headfirst entries like diving must be banned.

Above-ground pools are mostly purchased to beat the heat and are an affordable way to keep children happy during warm weather. Because large, spacious decks don't accompany all above-ground pools, there is not an abundance of poolside space for entertaining unless your backyard has a patio by the pool area or you build a large deck around it.

Perhaps the primary advantage of the above-ground pool is its price. If your budget is limited, this may be the pool for you. Some very nice above-ground pools can be installed for

Featuring a small deck and a security deck, this above-ground pool is quite affordable. Because they are relatively inexpensive, above-ground pools often serve as "starter" pools.

just a few thousand dollars; most often the prices range between $2,000 and $6,000. You can even erect these portable pools yourself, which will eliminate a hefty installation charge. Above-ground pools are often experiments for homeowners; if the portable pool experience is positive, they often eventually "graduate" to an in-ground pool.

Above-ground pools are most often constructed of steel or aluminum frames over which a vinyl liner is stretched. Large inflatable pools, which don't require any installation, are also growing in popularity. Because the pool sits above the ground, decking and landscaping around the pool can be important considerations, particularly if you don't want to look at bare pool walls. As you will see later, decking and landscaping will enhance the beauty of any pool. With the addition of these pleasing amenities, an above-ground pool can closely resemble its more expensive counterpart, the in-ground pool.

IN-GROUND POOLS

Before installing an in-ground pool, it is critical that you are clear on the following three points: the purpose of the pool, the main users of the pool, and your budget. Only after these points have been addressed should you begin to design the pool and the surrounding landscape.

Unlike above-ground pools—which are less expensive and often temporary structures—in-ground pools require excavation, are permanent, and, naturally, are more expensive. Although some above-ground pools may detract from a landscape, most in-ground pools enhance it. There are three basic options for in-ground pool construction: concrete, vinyl-lined, and fiberglass.

Concrete Pools   The major advantages of a concrete pool are permanence, durability, and flexibility in terms of design. Concrete pools, reinforced with steel rods to withstand the pressures of soil and water, are most often made of pneumatically applied concrete (gunite or shotcrete). Concrete pools can also be poured or made with masonry block. Although many pools can be installed within days, concrete pools may take weeks. The pool can be finished in plaster, paint, or tile—and all three come in a variety of colors.

A drawback of the in-ground concrete pool is its price—it is the most expensive of all pools. Costs generally begin at $10,000 and increase rapidly to $25,000 or more as the size and depth of the pool increases, due to higher material and

This guitar-shaped pool is interesting-looking and functional. Note the gradual walk-in entry at the neck, which is particularly nice for those who do not like or are unable to make an abrupt entry into the pool.

labor costs. Concrete pools cost more in colder climates because additional steel and concrete are needed to prevent the pool from shifting and cracking with freezing and warming temperatures.

Vinyl-Lined Pools

It was probably the advent of the vinyl-lined pool that made residential pools affordable for many homeowners. Vinyl-lined pools are much like vinyl flooring in that they can be made to look identical to tile. If you want a permanent pool but can't afford a concrete pool, you might want to investigate a vinyl-lined pool, an inexpensive and attractive alternative.

Vinyl-lined pools are placed into the ground in the same manner as concrete pools are, except that a flexible vinyl liner is stretched over the walls (which are made of steel, aluminum, wood, or similar noncorrosive material) instead of covering them with plaster, paint, or tile. The bottom of a vinyl-lined pool is usually compacted sand, which costs much less than concrete. Vinyl liners come in an array of attractive designs and colors, and are often custom cut for special applications. Cosmetically speaking, you'll have a difficult time telling the difference between a properly installed vinyl-lined pool and a concrete pool. And if you want to install a pool quickly, many vinyl-lined pools can be in place in less than a week.

Although vinyl-lined pools are durable, they don't last forever. The vinyl liner is quite resilient but may need to be replaced every ten years or so. (An average-size vinyl liner can be replaced for between $1,000 and $2,000.) Sharp objects can puncture the liner and cause leaking, but fortunately, you can patch these holes yourself. Unbalanced water chemistry, excessive chlorine, and sunlight can adversely affect the life of a vinyl liner as well, although vinyl liners that have sunlight and fungus inhibitors built into the material are also available.

The bottom line: while the cost and look of a vinyl liner are attractive, vinyl-lined pools cannot withstand the wear and tear that concrete pools can.

Fiberglass Pools

Fiberglass pools tend to fall between concrete pools and vinyl-lined pools in terms of price, durability, and longevity, so if you'd like a pool that is a little more enduring than the vinyl-lined variety but not as costly as concrete, a fiberglass pool could be the pool for you. These pools are typically prefabricated, made at a factory specifically for a particular site. Because they are constructed from molds, fiberglass pools are somewhat limited in size, shape, and availability in certain geographical locations. Transporting these pools is expensive, and they are rarely found far from population centers. Fiberglass pools, however, may present a few drawbacks.

But because of their slick surfaces, fiberglass pools are easy to clean and maintain—and this can be a big benefit for you. (When maintaining a fiberglass pool, make sure that you don't use abrasives or sharp instruments, or you'll scratch the finish.) Keeping the water balanced is also necessary, as the finish can be damaged in the presence of unbalanced water. As more pool builders produce fiberglass pools on the homeowner's site rather than in the factory, these durable pools will become more popular.

■ ■ ■

POOL DESIGNS

You can't build the perfect pool, that is, it's impossible to construct a pool that will support all aquatic activities—that's why water parks have so many different pools. The following are examples of pools that are becoming more popular around the world because of their appearance and function; most of these pool types are constructed of concrete.

This minimalistic pool and contemporary home complement each other well. The diving board has its own deep-water area, a nice safety feature found in public pools.

The Lap Pool

If fitness is a priority, a lap pool might be a good choice. Lap pools are long and narrow, with a minimum depth of 3 1/2 feet (1.1m) so that flip turns can be accommodated. Although lap pools can be as long as you wish (backyard permitting), they should be at least 40 feet (12.2m) long, although a length that is closer to 75 feet (22.9m) is preferable. The end walls must be parallel to each other and flat to provide a good surface from which to push off. The pool must be free of obstructions and hand rails. Ladders should be recessed in the side walls so that swimmers don't bump into them. A defined lap line should be painted or tiled on the bottom, and turning targets should be placed on the end walls to aid in reversing direction.

Some lap pools have standard-end walls and free-form side walls to accommodate other activities. The typical lap pool progresses from 3 1/2 feet in the shallow end to a depth of 5 feet (1.5m) in the deep end, but if the pool is going to be used for water aerobics, you'll only need approximately 4 feet (1.2m) of water.

The Reflecting Pool

If you want a pool that is used primarily for entertaining and relaxing rather than exercise, and is aesthetically pleasing, a geometric or free-form reflecting pool may be the best choice. A reflecting pool is not a reflecting pool in the literal sense, but is a swimming pool that is more often quiet than active with swimmers. Reflecting pools are mainly intended for aesthetics. In fact, what surrounds the pool may be more important than the pool itself. Barbecues, bars, gazebos, landscaping, gardens, and fountains are commonly found around this pool to promote relaxation.

Reflecting pools are more often shallow, usually between 3 1/2 and 5 feet (1.1 and 1.5m) deep, and normally don't have much equipment mounted on the pool deck. In general, reflecting pools tend to be larger and longer than most pools. Lighting is often used to highlight any of this pool's unusual features in the evening.

Colorful tiles interspersed among sections of lawn add interest to this long pool that does double-duty as a reflecting pool and lap pool.

This classic reflecting pool with attached spa has an open-air pool house, which allows for great views of the mountains in the distance from the pool house itself as well as from in the pool or on the pool deck.

The Naturalistic Pool

This is the pool for nature lovers. The emphasis here is on landscaping, in order to accomplish a dense, natural look. Both real and artificial stones and boulders can be strategically placed, and pool finishes can be painted dark to resemble the bottom of a lake or stream. Waterfalls are a common feature, and like the reflecting pool, the naturalistic pool is a place of relaxation. Lap swimming is not normally the primary activity, but if fitness swimming is desired, some sections can be constructed with flat walls and a straightaway of at least 40 feet (12m). The naturalistic pool can be an expensive undertaking, as it has many curves and contours as well as lush landscaping, both of which may drive the cost up.

The Waterscape

At first glance, waterscapes appear similar to naturalistic pools, but are in fact significantly different. A waterscape is a pool with many and varied attractions, often of grandiose proportions—the ultimate size is up to you. While these pools may be natural in design, they are planned with plenty of aquatic activity in mind, for adults and children alike. Waterscapes can create a backyard scene that more closely resembles a beautiful natural aquatic setting rather than a swimming pool. Many waterscapes can be designed for a variety of children's activities (sliding, jumping, splashing) and separate adult activities (bathing in the spa, tanning, and so on). Another way to help distinguish between a naturalistic pool and a waterscape is to look at the price tag: waterscapes are much more expensive.

Some popular features often found in naturalistic waterscapes include waterfalls, water slides, bridges, fountains, hot-water spas, grottoes, and even beaches. Elaborate landscaping and dramatic lighting are a vital part of these pool packages. In fact, with the right lighting, many of these pools can be even more beautiful during the evening.

The Vanishing-Edge Pool

The vanishing-edge pool is a very popular new pool design that is most often used to enhance a combined view of the pool and an ocean, lake, or valley beyond the pool. The visual trick is to design the pool edge so that no walls or deck are evident between the pool and the view behind the pool. In this manner, the pool and the background become one, for a truly outstanding effect. Vanishing-edge pools work well overlooking land, but when they are placed to overlook an ocean or bay, it is often difficult to differentiate between the pool water and the open water.

Top left: Dense landscaping enhances the natural look of this waterscape and insures privacy by hiding the pool from view. Top right: This blue lagoon, complete with a walk-in beach and palm trees, blends in perfectly with the landscape. Right: This vanishing-edge pool offers spectacular views of the ocean as well as a cool reprieve from the sun. The terra-cotta walkway connects the house and pool.

Vanishing-edge pools work best on a slope or hilltop, so if your property overlooks an appealing vista, this might be a good choice. But because they are usually built on slopes, vanishing-edge pools require more structural support, and because each pool is custom-designed and built to highlight the views, vanishing-edge pools are generally expensive to build. Long, narrow pools are the most common shape, as this is the most effective way to accentuate the vanishing edge.

Spas More and more people are incorporating hot-water spas into the layout of their swimming pools. A spa makes a pool more flexible in terms of use by allowing for hot-water relaxation and therapy in or near a cool-water pool setting, particularly for those who don't consider themselves swimmers. In fact, the cost of installing a spa along with a pool is usually much less than when the spa is built separately from the pool. For more information on the variety of spas available today, see chapter three.

■ ■ ■

CONSTRUCTION DETAILS

When homeowners imagine a pool in their backyards, they usually visualize the finished product: a shimmering blue oasis, the centerpiece of their property. But if this pool is going to be functional and problem-free, the layout and construction details must be considered carefully with the pool builder. Unfortunately, most homeowners do not want to be involved with this stage of the project, which is perhaps the most important step in terms of the successful completion of the

Contrasting styles. Left: A large, free-form pool with natural outcroppings resembles a lake in the backyard. Below: This contemporary pool with straight lines and raised spa is a no-nonsense pool designed for pool buffs.

pool. It's embarrassing and frustrating when a backyard is converted to a swamp because of poor drainage, or when the corner of a pool is actually placed in someone else's yard. Spend a lot of time planning this portion of the project—because if you're not pleased with your pool's performance after a year or so, unlike a car, you cannot trade it in.

Once it has been decided where the pool will be placed in the yard and good drainage has been guaranteed, the skimmers, inlets, and filtration equipment must be strategically placed for good circulation and disinfection. This is not an area in which to cut costs because the efficiency of the pool's functioning will be compromised. Many pool builders attempt to become the low bidder on a pool job by eliminating "unnecessary" items. It's true that plumbing costs can be greatly reduced by decreasing the number of skimmers and outlets or by placing these features close to the pool pump, but it's also true that this may adversely affect circulation, filtration, and disinfection.

Bottom contours and finishes must also be carefully considered before this phase of the project is complete. Whenever a doubt is raised about the strength of pool walls and floors, more steel reinforcement and concrete should be added. If the pool budget must be reduced, cut back on landscaping, pool furniture, and other areas rather than pool construction, because once the pool is built, it is almost impossible to correct any structural problems. You can always buy a grill.

Just after your pool contractor places his pins and lines on your lawn to mark the excavation, and just before his equipment begins to dig up your yard, do one final walk-about with your builder to reassure yourself of the placement of the main drain, pool inlets and skimmers, entry and exit points, and filter location. This will help to safeguard you from panicking when the excavation begins.

Drainage

In order to obtain proper drainage, some pool builders recommend that the top of the pool be several feet (about 1m) above the highest grade in the area. If this can be done, there is little chance that surface runoff water will find its way back into the pool. With many pools, however, this may not be possible, but if the pool deck is kept 3 to 4 inches (7.6 to 10.2cm) above the ground surrounding it, water will probably run off from the pool without re-entering it. The soil around the pool must also be stable and provide good drainage, both on- and under-ground so as not to delay construction. If the soil has poor drainage, there are many methods of improving it. This process, however, will increase costs.

Site Development and Construction Evaluation: A Checklist

■ **Building codes and zoning laws:** get these in writing from your zoning or code office.

■ **Standards and health codes for swimming pools:** check with your municipality for swimming pool requirements and safety considerations. These vary significantly between localities.

■ **Building permit:** complete all required paperwork and secure a building permit. This is the homeowner's responsibility.

■ **Access to site:** speak with the contractor and your neighbors to determine how the site will be accessed.

■ **Exact location of your pool:** plan convenient access for pool users while avoiding overhead and underground obstructions.

■ **Soil, grade, and drainage:** study the grade to provide good drainage and stable soil for excavation. Your builder must help you here.

■ **Advanced knowledge of subsoil conditions:** be aware of existing conditions. Who pays when excavation is hampered?

■ **Skimmer and return placement:** carefully place these to provide good circulation and disinfection.

■ **Pump and filter location:** place equipment carefully: neither too close nor too far from the pool—25 to 50 feet (7.6 to 15.2m) is best. The equipment should be placed on a concrete slab but landscaped well so that it is camouflaged.

Construction Tips

■ **Beware of dirt walks:** whenever dirt must be moved by hand (shovel and wheelbarrow), excavation costs will increase considerably.

■ **Add steel and concrete:** steep grades and unstable soil conditions require lots of additional steel reinforcing rods and concrete. You'll need to add these items, but you'll have to pay a hefty sum for doing so.

■ **Extra, extra:** I usually recommend extra skimmers, inlets, underwater lights, love seats, ladders, and the like for most pools because they significantly improve the entire project. Unfortunately, extras cost extra.

■ **Compare apples to apples:** many low bidders keep the cost of the pool down by shortcutting the plumbing (insufficient skimmers and inlets) or by using cheaper equipment. When comparing construction costs, be certain that the bids include identical equipment.

■ **Don't cope too soon:** coping stones and tiles should not be set until the pool shell has cured for about a week.

■ **Don't rush the deck:** Pool builders are often asked to expand the size of the deck at the last minute. Consider a larger deck before the contractor begins to pour it. Make sure the deck will meet your needs.

■ **Beware of subs:** if a pool builder uses too many subcontractors for certain trades (electrical, plumbing, plastering, etc.), he can lose control of the project. Many homeowners feel more comfortable with a pool contractor who does most of the work himself and is on the site most of the time.

■ **Buy from a builder, not a salesperson:** be wary of those who sell pools that someone else builds. Although they may have good intentions, pool sellers on commission often don't have the answers to your questions and don't know what works well and what doesn't.

Inlet and Skimmer Placement

As soon as the pool builder has dug a hole in your yard, he will begin to install piping and plumbing. At this point, be certain that inlets, which inject the pool with treated water, and skimmers, which return dirty water to the filter, are placed strategically. A minimum of two skimmers is recommended; if there is only one skimmer, it should be placed on the long side of the pool and downwind of prevailing breezes. If placed in this manner, the skimmer will catch most of the surface debris. If the pool is to be vacuumed from the skimmers, be sure that they are centrally located so that both ends of the pool can be vacuumed easily. (Beware: some builders will install only one skimmer in order to reduce costs and labor.)

Inlets should be placed carefully to ensure that pool disinfectants are evenly distributed and that "dead spots" (areas where water is not well circulated and disinfected, which can lead to bacteria and algae growth) are not created.

It is important to discuss inlet and skimmer placement with your pool builder before he installs the plumbing. Some pool contractors will place these vital components wherever it is easiest or cheapest to install them, not where they should be placed for optimum water circulation.

Filter Location

As with inlets and skimmers, it is important to discuss the location of the pool filter, pump, and associated equipment with the contractor prior to construction. Poor placement of the pool filter will not only clutter your landscape but work inefficiently. For aesthetics, the pool recirculation equipment should be hidden from view by appropriate landscaping or other screening. In addition, the equip-

This stately contemporary home and pool strike the perfect balance. Placing the pool at a diagonal to the large staircase (left) evens out the visual weight of the landscape.

ment cannot be located too far from the pool because the pump may lose power trying to push water across a great distance. If placed too far from the pool, the equipment will also be inconvenient for you to operate because of the long trip between the pool and the pump. Don't place the filtration equipment too close to the pool, either: not only is it not particularly attractive, it is also somewhat noisy. Generally, 25 to 50 feet (7.6 to 15.2m) is ideal.

Finishes

The finish of a swimming pool is a critical feature that must be chosen with care. Pool finishes should not only look good but be nonslip, watertight, durable, and easily maintained. There are many advantages and disadvantages of each type of finish, but typically, the more durable the finish,

the more expensive it will be. It is important to keep pool chemicals and water balance at levels compatible with the pool finish, for a pool disinfectant level in a pool with one finish may not be compatible in another.

Tile

Tile is the most expensive finish, but it is also the most durable (it is practically indestructible) and most versatile. A tile pool costs about $15 to $20 a square foot ($161 to $645 a sq m). Tile is most compatible with concrete pools.

Tile can be used to accent special features inside the pool shell. Darker tiles can be used to line bottom contours, as well as the edges of steps and slopes. Beautiful tile mosaics in almost any motif can also be added to the pool bottom and walls to customize the pool finish.

Tile is more than a durable finish: it's one way to add a colorful, individual touch to your project. This seaside plaster pool features a whimsical mosaic whirlpool at the foot of the steps, and the dividing line stretching along the bottom mimics the contours of the coastline that runs parallel to the pool.

Plaster Many concrete pools are finished with plasters like Marcite or Marblelite. These plaster finishes offer nonslip surfaces that last for many years. Plaster finishes are much less expensive than tile and provide a beautiful finish. A plaster pool costs about $3 to $4 a square foot ($32 to $129 a sq m). Plaster finishes may be more prone to staining, particularly from heavy metals like iron (red) and copper (blue-green) that may be present in your water source or makeup. Many pool owners combine tile finishes and plaster by using tiles to high-

light the water line, steps, and contours, or to mark lap lanes, thereby obtaining the beauty of tile without the high cost of a fully tiled pool.

Paint A pool can be painted with great results. If you decide to paint your pool, use either chlorinated rubber-based or epoxy paints. Chlorinated rubber-based paints are resistant to pool chemicals and unbalanced water, and are popular for

Swimming for Special Populations

Special ramps and lifts are available for elderly or disabled swimmers. Certainly, swimming provides great exercise and therapy for all individuals but especially for those who cannot engage in everyday exercise. When a physician prescribes water therapy, and the pool is used specifically for this purpose, the cost of the pool and specialized equipment may be deducted as a medical expense on income tax returns. Consult your lawyer or accountant before claiming this deduction, however.

A work of art, this pool incorporates manufactured walls, windows, and screens to create effects with light and to add color to the poolscape.

pool renovation projects. Epoxy paints are expensive, but they create a hard impervious surface.

Painted pool finishes generally last about five years. When painting a pool, it is imperative that the manufacturer's recommendations be followed. All surfaces should be thoroughly cleaned, scraped, and dried. In addition, pools must be painted only when the weather will permit proper drying and curing time. Without sufficient curing time, paint may be dry to the touch but wet underneath. Peeling and chipping will result if paint is not allowed sufficient time to cure. Many pool paints require five to seven additional days of curing time after the paint dries, and only after that should the swimming pool be filled with water.

Vinyl Lining and Fiberglass   These two construction materials are considered pool finishes and are discussed on page 52.

Digesting this chapter is probably similar to what a child experiences when walking through a toy store—there's just too much to choose from. Don't dismay: your reasons for wanting a pool will greatly assist you in the selection process. For example, fitness buffs tend to prefer lap pools, those who frequently entertain gravitate toward reflecting pools, and families with children are attracted to waterscapes. But selecting the correct style of pool is only the beginning of a long but rewarding search. Be a stickler for details in determining your pool's size, shape, depth, contours, and finishes; remember, do not cut back in these vital areas, regardless of finances.

Chapter Three

Spas and Hot Tubs

THE ROMANS, THE JAPANESE, AND COUNTLESS OTHER PEOPLES have enjoyed the benefits of hot-water immersions throughout history, and now you can, too. Soaking in a hot-water pool relaxes tired muscles, promotes circulation, and helps relieve mental stress. Additionally, many professional athletes use hydrotherapy and hot baths for rehabilitation. Fortunately, spas and hot tubs are much less expensive to purchase and operate than traditional swimming pools, and if a hot water tub or spa is purchased for prescribed therapy, it's probably tax-deductible. Spas and hot tubs have become a vital component of health clubs, hotels, and private residences. In fact, homeowners who add a hot tub or spa often feel that it is their most valuable home improvement.

Although many people think that swimming pools are quite similar to hot tubs and spas, there are major differences between them. A significant difference is water temperature. When the water temperature in a swimming pool becomes greater than 90°F (32.2°C), it is technically

What's the Difference Between a Hot Tub and a Spa?

"Hot tub," "spa," "whirlpool," and "jacuzzi" are just a few of the terms that have been used interchangeably over the years to describe hot-water specialty pools. The basic difference between hot tubs and spas is that hot tubs are made of wood and spas are not. Spas can be constructed of concrete, fiberglass, acrylic, or other synthetic materials. Whirlpool is the term that is used to describe the swirling action of the water in therapy pools, and Jacuzzi is the brand name that identifies certain manufactured pool parts such as pumps, jets, and filters.

Brick and wood can be tastefully combined, evidenced by this well-placed spa.

considered a spa (the average swimming pool temperature should be 78° to 82°F [25.5° to 27.8°C]). Hot tubs and spas do not produce significant hot-water benefits until the temperature is above 89°F (31.6°C). Generally, hot tubs and spas maintain water temperatures between 99° and 104°F (37.2° and 40°C). Any pool with water temperatures greater than 104°F can be dangerous, as this can cause unconsciousness, for starters. Excessively hot water can also cause body temperatures to rise quickly, affect blood pressure, and cause drowsiness. A fifteen-minute timer switch on the jets and blowers should help prevent soakers from staying in the water too long.

In addition to hot water, hot tubs and spas are equipped with high-pressure air and water jets that have a massaging effect—another feature that differentiates them from swimming pools. Although hot tubs and spas are emptied infrequently, it is important that they be emptied more often than swimming pools because the water in these smaller vessels receives relatively more contaminants. (In larger pools, the contaminants are diluted in larger volumes of water and therefore go unnoticed.)

Whereas swimming pools offer a variety of water activities, hot tubs and spas focus on inactivity. When you enter a hot-water pool, you do so simply to sit and relax. Built-in benches are provided and physical activity should actually be discouraged; high temperatures combined with physical exertion can lead to accidents.

The ingredients for a successful hot tub or spa are quite simple: hot water that is chemically balanced and filtered, sufficient seats or benches for all participants, an adequate number of jets, an underwater light for ambience and safety, and more than one bottom outlet (drain). Another amenity that will greatly enhance your hot-water experience is a nearby shower, which will enable you to wash before and after using the hot-water pool. Soap showers not only keep the water and shell clean, but also help prevent the passing of germs and bacteria to others using the hot tub or spa. When placed indoors, reinforced floors are a must, for most spas and hot tubs produce a weight that is five times greater than most floors can support safely.

■ ■ ■

HOT TUBS

Hot-tubbing as we know it today became popular in California during the late 1960s. More specifically, Santa Barbarans who enjoyed soaking in nearby canyon hot springs combined the watertight, wooden wine barrels from California's wine country with modern technology to reproduce hot springs on their own properties. Wine barrels and caskets are available in a variety of sizes, although just about all are round. Therefore, a hot tub is technically a wooden tub filled with hot water and hydrotherapy jets. Hot tubs can be made of redwood, mahogany, teak, cedar, and other woods. Hot tubs may be placed either outside or inside your home and can cost anywhere between $5,000 and $8,000.

When a hot tub is first filled, the water will probably turn brown. This rust- or coffee-colored water is produced by the tannic acid in the wood that is leaching out into the water. Consequently, it is imperative that new hot tubs be filled and emptied frequently during the first month of ownership—or until this discoloration stops completely. New hot tubs also tend to leak slightly until the wood eventually swells and becomes watertight.

If you prefer a deeper tub and a rustic look, you may also prefer a hot tub to a spa, although a hot tub will require more maintenance and is somewhat harder to keep clean. As far as drainage is concerned, hot tubs require more care; if drained for more than a day or two, the wood will shrink, causing the tub to leak when refilled. Whenever you dump your tub, do it for a short period of time. Water chemistry is also a more crucial factor in hot tubs than in spas. Insufficient disinfection can allow bacteria to grow at a faster rate in the porous surfaces of the wood. Conversely, excessive disinfection can cause the wood to discolor.

■ ■ ■

SPAS

If you prefer soaking in a slick, shiny vessel and want less maintenance, consider installing a spa. A spa is simply a modern version of the rustic hot tub. Instead of wood, spas are composed of concrete and tile, fiberglass, acrylic, thermoplastic, or stainless steel. Spas are often prefabricated shells that come in a variety of shapes, sizes, and colors, and with various seating arrangements. Spas can be installed in-ground or above-ground, inside or outside. Electrical safety is an important concern, whether the spa is above-ground and portable or in-ground and permanent. Spas are generally easier to keep clean than hot tubs because their slick surfaces can be quickly wiped clean when they become dirty or greasy.

Portable Spas

Above-ground spas are portable and easy to move because they are self-contained—all of their circulation equipment is hidden underneath the skirt, or frame. The average portable spa weighs 300 to 500 pounds (135 to 225kg) and normally holds 100 to 500 gallons (380 to 1,900l) of water. Despite their weight, portable spas can usually be moved on their sides through a doorway. Because they are temporary structures, they do not normally require a building permit, nor do they require any construction, although they usually need to be placed on a reinforced floor for support.

The price of the above-ground spa is tempting as well; many portable spas can be purchased for as little as $3,500—far less than the cost of the deeper, in-ground spa.

The portable spa is usually heated by electricity, and many models only require 110 volts, which can be obtained in any residential wall outlet. A portable spa should, however, be on a 20-amp circuit by itself, without other large appliances. Otherwise, you'll blow the circuit.

One disadvantage of a portable spa on 110 volts is that it is slow to heat up. To combat this problem, you might consider having an electrician hard-wire the spa for 220 volts. A spa running on 220 volts will heat up much more quickly but will be less portable because of the hard wiring.

In-Ground Spas

In-ground spas are permanent installations. In-ground spas are also typically more expensive—they cost roughly $6,000 to $8,000. Their circulation equipment is not self-contained but located nearby, often in an adjacent room or closet. Purchasing an in-ground spa is usually a more involved process than a portable spa because

design, planning, construction, and landscaping are often part of the package. Most large, in-ground commercial spas are made of concrete. Smaller concrete spas are also available, and can be installed indoors or out. Although concrete spas are durable and easy to maintain, installing one is similar to building a swimming pool. Concrete spas are custom-poured, thereby adding considerable expense for labor, materials, and specialized equipment. Residential in-ground concrete spas tend to be large, elaborate, and expensive, but they last forever. Concrete spas can be lined with indestructible tile to make maintenance easy, or if this is too costly, a ring of tile may be placed at water level to aid in cleaning the scum line. Cleaning the scum line from concrete is extremely difficult.

The most popular in-ground spas are made of acrylic, fiberglass, or other high-tech plastics. These plastics are much less expensive than tile and concrete, and their finishes are beautiful, but extra care must be taken to avoid scratching them. Proper water balance is more essential in these spas to protect the finish.

Swim Spas
Perhaps the most recent development in this area of spas is the swim spa, which can be installed indoors or out. Generally rectangular, most swim spas are longer than spas and hot tubs but much shorter than most swimming pools. Swim spas fulfill two functions. If you wish to lap-swim for exercise without committing the space or money to build a long pool (65 to 75 feet [19.8 to 22.9m]), the swim spa allows you to swim in place just as a treadmill allows you to jog in

This hot tub blends in perfectly with the wooden exterior of this suburban home and its extensive naturalistic landscaping.

place. A large swim spa can be 10 × 20 feet (3 × 6.1m) long. For fitness swimming, temperatures should be maintained between 78° and 82°F (25.5° and 27.8°C). The water current in the spa can be adjusted to your strength, conditioning, and skill level; if you want to increase the intensity of your workout, simply turn up the current.

The second function of the swim spa is relaxation and hydromassage. The thermostat may be adjusted to increase the water temperature so that when you are not swimming vigorously in place, you can relax by soaking in the same way as hot tubbers do. Some larger swim spas have separate swimming and soaking areas so that swimmers can enjoy different activities simultaneously.

■ ■ ■

INSTALLING THE SPA

Once you've decided which type of hot tub or spa meets your needs, you'll need to consider whether to install it in your home or outdoors. Here are important tips to bear in mind.

Outdoor Spas
Outdoor hot tubs and spas either can be incorporated into an existing swimming pool design or installed independently. But no matter what you do, all local and zoning ordinances must be understood and followed before placing a hot tub or spa outdoors.

Whenever possible, a hot-water pool located in or adjacent to a larger, traditional pool should contain its own pump and filter because circulation, filtration, and chemical requirements for hot tubs and spas are much more stringent than those for swimming pools.

A spa's placement in the yard is an important consideration. If you live in a warm climate, putting the hot tub or spa in the shade is not a bad idea because the combination of hot air and hot water can be intolerable at times. In colder climates, outdoor hot tubs and spas need all the direct sunlight they can get to keep soakers warm. But even in colder climates, many outdoor hot tubs and spas can be used year-round. (Never quickly enter a cool pool directly from a hot tub or spa, as your body may be shocked by the sudden, dramatic temperature change.)

In addition, many homeowners enjoy hot-tubbing in private; privacy can be achieved with landscaping or with a trellis or gazebo. Some spas are separated from the swimming pool with glass block; this style is becoming more popular and is very attractive. Lounging areas and seating outside these pools are also nice conveniences for those waiting their turn to enter the spa or hot tub.

As is true with swimming pools, spa decking and walkways must be nonslip and have good drainage. Outdoor spas and hot tubs must be covered for safety, for water and heat conservation, and also to keep out debris. Fencing (see chapter six) is essential for safety and security reasons as well.

Indoor Spas
There are many attractive ways to install a hot tub or spa indoors. Walls of glass, stone, or wood will enhance any indoor hot tub or spa setting. The hot-water pool can also serve as the center of an indoor garden for a greenhouse effect. An indoor spa with a great outdoor view is a nice idea, too. The hot tub can serve as an extension of a bedroom, recreation room, or fitness center. Some people even add a special room to their house for the spa.

Twin spas. Here, the upper, hot water spa spills over into the lower, cool water spa, allowing soakers to alternate between the two in true Swedish spa tradition. Three attractive spillways adjoin the spas, while removable stainless steel handrails facilitate getting in and out of the water.

If the installation of the hot tub is not planned properly, however, moisture and unpleasant odors can invade the rest of the home. It is absolutely essential for excellent ventilation to be available in the room that houses the hot tub or spa. If excellent ventilation does not exist in your home, condensation will form on nearby windows, obscuring views and causing damage to furnishings. Roof vents or exhaust fans may be added to help control humidity and odors. Floor drains, non-slip flooring, a reinforced floor (consult a professional contractor to determine how much reinforcement to the existing floor is necessary), rust-resistant fixtures, and covers are crucial to insuring a safe and enjoyable indoor spa. Moisture-loving plants will add beauty to the spa environment.

COVERS

You should always cover your spa or hot tub when you're not using it. Covers, which can be made of fiberglass, canvas, plastic, or wood, have many important advantages. Covers can keep debris out of the water; keep children out, therefore providing an important measure of safety; significantly reduce heating costs; and significantly reduce the evaporation of water and chemicals.

Most spa and hot tub dealers agree that safety covers should be a part of every hot-water package. If you're interested in cutting corners to save money on your hot tub or spa installation, don't skimp on the cover because it will ultimately cost you more. For additional energy conservation, your hot tub or spa may be turned off when you're not using it. However, every spa and hot tub should be filtering, heating, and disinfecting the water—usually for twenty to thirty minutes—before, during, and after each use. Also see Covers in chapter six on page 128.

■ ■ ■

HOT-WATER CIRCULATION SYSTEMS

Although their circulation systems are similar to those of swimming pools, spas have smaller components located under or adjacent to the shell. In addition to the filter, pump, heater, and chemical feeder, most hot tubs and spas have hydrojets, and some have air blowers. Hydrojets produce a massaging action, and air blowers provide a tingling flow of bubbles into the hot-water pool. All this equipment is included in the portable spa package and is called a skid pack. All equipment should pass the stringent requirements of an independent testing laboratory.

■ ■ ■

HOT-WATER CHEMISTRY

There are special challenges when dealing with hot-water chemistry. The hot water and the turbulence created by the hydrotherapy jets present unique chemical problems for the spa or hot-tub owner. Basically, disinfectants used to keep the water clean and clear are unstable at higher temperatures.

Rustic elegance is provided by this traditional wooden hot tub. It is natural, functional, and relatively inexpensive, and takes up very little space—ideal for homeowners with small yards.

Bromine, for instance, is more popular in hot-water applications than chlorine because bromine is more stable at elevated temperatures. The hydrotherapy jets also aerate and move water, causing some of the disinfectant to come out of the solution. Evaporation is also greater when the jets are turned on, thereby increasing chemical loss. In summary, it takes greater diligence to keep chemical levels up in a spa than in a pool.

In addition, several people in a hot tub or spa can tax the disinfection and filtration system, for most people perspire profusely while in a hot tub or spa. Because relatively more perspiration finds its way into a small pool, a relatively greater amount of disinfectant is needed to keep the water clean. Recommended chemical levels for a hot tub or spa are almost double that required for a swimming pool. Also, as the free, active disinfectants combine with natural body by-products, they can create unpleasant odors and eye irritation. One way

Top: This large, spacious in-ground spa offers plenty of room for sitting and lounging while soaking. Large groups can be accommodated easily in this spa, and the vegetation softens the spa's geometric shape. Bottom: A wood deck and wall enhance the natural beauty of this wooden hot tub, while the hard-top safety cover prevents accidents.

of attacking this problem is to "shock," or superchlorinate, the water (see chapter five) with high dosages of chemicals; another alternative is to drain and clean the spa or hot tub regularly. Provided there are no water restrictions in place, you may find dumping the spa or hot tub to be more effective and less expensive—and healthier—than superchlorination.

■ ■ ■

SAFETY

Although soaking in a spa or hot tub is usually associated with health and vigor, some people should refrain from using them. Don't use a spa or hot tub if you have one of the following conditions, or unless hot-water hydrotherapy has been recommended by a physician.

■ Persons with ailments such as heart disease, diabetes, high or low blood pressure, or any other serious illness must consult a doctor before entering a spa or hot tub.

■ Pregnant women should also avoid the use of spas and hot tubs. The fetus can be adversely affected by the high water temperatures.

■ Children should never be allowed to soak without adult supervision. Many hot tubs and spas are reserved for persons twelve and older. Children who are allowed to use spas and hot tubs must not be permitted to jump, dive, or swim underwater. Such activity can result in the entanglement of limbs and hair in bottom drains. For this reason, all drains and bottom outlets must be covered with antivortex plates.

In addition, certain conditions in and around the hot tub or spa may pose a hazard and should be removed before using the tub or spa. Some of these safety concerns are:

■ Do not use the hot tub or spa when the bottom cannot be clearly seen from the deck. If an accident should occur, rescue efforts would be significantly impaired in cloudy water.

■ Never use a hot tub or spa when the antivortex plates are not in place over the bottom outlets. As mentioned regarding safety for children, bottom outlets without safety covers create tremendous suction and can entrap hair and limbs on the bottom, and that goes for people of all ages. Modern hot tubs and spas should be equipped with two bottom outlets; doing so reduces the chance of entrapment because the return suction is spread out over two openings.

■ All electrical appliances including the telephone must be kept a minimum of 5 feet (1.5m) away from the spa. Handling any electrical device in the water can lead to electrocution. This includes hair dryers and video and stereo equipment. All electrical outlets must be covered and protected by Ground Fault Interrupters (GFI).

■ Persons with external infections and wounds should not enter the water. Likewise, soaking should be avoided when the water chemistry and filtration are less than ideal. This is because many bacteria thrive at higher water temperatures. To make matters worse, the pores of the body dilate in hot water and accept bacteria more readily. Spas and hot tubs with less than impeccable water chemistry and filtration can easily transmit infections from one soaker to another.

■ Avoid drugs and alcohol. High water temperature coupled with drugs and alcohol can lead to unconsciousness, which may in turn lead to drowning. If drinking is a must in a hot tub or spa, ice water or chilled fruit juices are recommended.

■ Glass must never be used in and around a hot tub or spa. Use plastic or paper cups to avoid breakage.

■ When not in use, spas and hot tubs should be covered and secured with a fence or locked door. Small children must be prevented from entering the spa or hot tub unsupervised.

■ When your hot tub is installed, make certain that it includes an emergency switch that shuts the system off. Rescue efforts will be made easier in the event of entrapment or some other problem if the pumps can be quickly shut down.

Spas at a Glance

Spa Type	Cost
Portable spa	
Acrylic/thermoplastic	$3,500–$8,000
Custom-built spa (detached from pool)	
Acrylic/thermoplastic	$5,000–$8,000
Concrete/gunite	$6,000–$10,000
Wooden hot tub	$5,000–$8,000
Custom-built spa (attached to pool with shared filtration)	
Concrete/gunite	$4,000–$8,000

This attached spa is a subtle, elegant addition to this natural poolscape. Both the wooden deck and potted flowers blend in well with the setting and enhance the pool and spa.

■ ■ ■

PURCHASING A SPA OR HOT TUB

Spa and hot-tub dealers should be listed in the telephone directory: determine which ones are members of the Better Business Bureau or other reputable trade organization that sets standards for hot-water specialty pools. Spas and hot tubs should be the dealer's full-time business or part of a larger swimming pool business. Since the industry is still quite young, some dealers are still experimenting with spas and hot tubs as a sideline; some have been successful but many have failed. Most homeowners should avoid dealers that are earning while learning the trade. Check the background of the dealer thoroughly, particularly regarding years in the business, references, and product line. Before signing a contract, get as much information as possible about the dealer. Checking on several references and visiting several installations will probably be of the most value to you.

Before signing a contract, make sure warranties are included with the purchase that cover the spa shell (two to five years), supporting structures (five years), cover (five years), and pump, filter, heater, and blowers (one year). Be sure you completely understand the length of the warranty and type of coverage it offers for every item. All equipment should have an Underwriters Laboratory (UL) or a similar testing standard marked on its label.

Entertaining, exercising, and relaxation can all be enhanced with a hot tub or spa. The benefits of hot-water soaking are immeasurable, and soaking in a private spa is much safer than soaking in a public one. If you follow the suggestions in this chapter, adding a hot tub or spa to your home will provide hours of safe and enjoyable relaxation without a high price tag or taking up much space. Although selecting the most appropriate hot tub or spa can be difficult, it certainly is less complicated than choosing a pool. In most cases, if you're not completely satisfied, you may be able to trade the spa for an upgraded model.

Chapter Four

Case Studies

BEFORE PURCHASING A NEW POOL OR SPA OR RENOVATING AN OLD one, it is essential to know what the process is going to cost. Determining the cost of a pool or spa alone is relatively easy, but it is often difficult to figure out the cost of the entire pool installation with all the extras. The reason this is difficult is that while the cost of the pool itself is obvious, there are many variables and many necessary additions—fencing, decking, covers, and so on—and many optional ones—alarms, landscaping, automated systems, and so on. These options vary widely in price and are a separate cost from the pool package. Too often it's even difficult to determine what equipment you actually need. This chapter is meant to help you in that regard by presenting pool project comparisons.

Representative of the broad swimming pool market, the case studies presented here are organized in a progressive manner, moving from basic, inexpensive starter models to elaborate, expensive projects with all the trimmings. In general, as the selected pools increase in size and grandeur, landscaping and other amenities tend to become more elaborate—hence costs increase as well. Since pool pricing varies widely throughout the world and is inevitably apt to change, each pool is relatively rated below on a sliding scale to indicate approximate costs.

APPROXIMATE POOL PRICES	
($)	less than $10,000
($$)	$10,000–$20,000
($$$)	$20,000–$50,000
($$$$)	$50,000–$100,000
($$$$$)	$100,000+

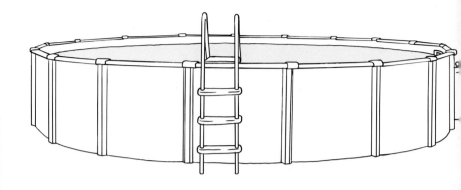

A basic, circular above-ground pool is inexpensive to purchase and easy to install; many homeowners can do it themselves.

ABOVE-GROUND POOLS

Above-ground pools may not be the most gorgeous residential pool packages, but they are extremely popular and deserve a brief mention. Homeowners who purchase above-ground pools do so because it is an inexpensive way to beat the heat and because property excavation usually is not necessary. Above-ground pools appeal to first-time owners because they are affordable and convenient; they offer clear, clean water; and they can often be installed by the owners themselves. Extras like decking and landscaping are not part of the package. Not surprisingly, the above-ground pool is often referred to as a "starter" pool, particularly for young families with small children. Most above-ground pools cost very little, between $1,500 and $3,000.

While less expensive than other models, an above-ground pool probably won't add to the value of a house, offers little flexibility in size and design, has a limited life span, and, if not

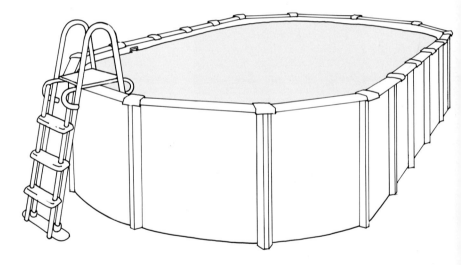

A rectangular above-ground pool offers more room to swim than a circular above-ground pool. For safety reasons, when an above-ground pool is not in use, its ladder should be removed to avoid accidents.

dressed up, may not be the most attractive choice. But for those homeowners who are not totally convinced that a pool is right for them or who want to experience pool ownership without going into debt, the above-ground pool may be a safe bet.

There are several options that should be considered when contemplating the purchase of an above-ground pool:

A retractable ladder. This can be purchased for easy access when the pool is in use, but can also be easily removed for safety when the pool is closed.

"No Diving" signs and labels. These should be placed directly on the walls, top rail, and ladder, as headfirst entries in above-ground pools are dangerous.

Inexpensive privacy and/or security fences. These can be attached to the top rail of the pool.

Decking, ladders, slides, and other amenities. The exposed walls of an above-ground pool are sufficiently sturdy to allow for the attachment of such options, but the real beauty of this particular pool is that it can be enjoyed as is, without all the extras.

A custom deck. This can be added to the perimeter of most above-ground pools to accommodate more poolside activities while camouflaging the pool walls at the same time.

Landscaping. Installing medium-size shrubs adjacent to the pool walls can dress up the pool and soften its appearance when installing decking is not possible.

Gravel or stone placed on the ground outside the pool directly adjacent to the pool walls. This provides for good drainage and a nonslip surface.

Elaborate, Above-Ground Pool with Spa

($ or $$) This pool project was undertaken by the builders to illustrate how an inexpensive above-ground pool can be installed to look like an expensive in-ground pool with all the extras. And the builders were quite successful—this project demonstrates how homeowners can divert money saved on the purchase of an above-ground pool toward the enhancement of the entire backyard.

Perhaps the most noteworthy trait of this pool project is the beautiful redwood decking and fencing. Notice how the latticework on top of the fence adds interest and beauty to what would otherwise be a nondescript feature. The pool and spa, which are nicely tucked into a far corner of the yard, can be reached directly through the French doors in the master bedroom of the house. The pool also has a built-in bar, which is hidden under the pool deck. The landscaping consists primarily of container plantings, which reduces maintenance and allows the owners to add and remove plants as they wish.

Another nice aesthetic touch is the large shade tree around which the deck is constructed. The pool itself is engulfed in shade, which may keep both pool water and swimmers cool—both a potential benefit and a hindrance.

Cost-cutting measures could include eliminating the bar and/or the spa, or reducing the size of the deck. It should be emphasized that although the lovely redwood deck really makes this project complete, it eventually may require additional maintenance due to weathering. The large shade tree is also a potential problem. Maintaining the pool and spa would be laborious, particularly if the tree needed to be pruned or if it dropped a great deal of leaves. The other drawbacks are the above-ground pool's inherent limited size, shape, and life span.

Beautiful redwood decking and fencing transform this very affordable above-ground pool into an attractive in-ground look-alike. Purchasing an above-ground pool enabled its owners to avoid excavation and construction costs, thus allowing them to spend more on amenities, such as a spa and a spacious deck.

SPECIAL FEATURES

■ This pool project is very affordable.

■ Beautiful redwood decking and fencing add considerably to the pool's elegant look.

■ The pool was dug 2 feet (0.6m) into the ground to make it look like an in-ground pool.

■ A spa is located on the deck near the pool, making it easy to go back and forth between the two.

■ A built-in bar is hidden under the deck.

■ The pool is accessible through the master bedroom.

■ Although an above-ground pool, this project should add to the value of the house.

IN-GROUND VINYL-LINED AND FIBERGLASS POOLS

The development of vinyl-lined pools made in-ground pools more affordable for many homeowners, as vinyl-lined pools are less expensive than concrete pools in terms of labor and materials. In fact, some in-ground vinyl-lined pools can be purchased for half the price of an in-ground concrete pool. Many vinyl-lined pools can be purchased and installed for less than $12,000—but extras can increase costs quickly. Fiberglass pools,

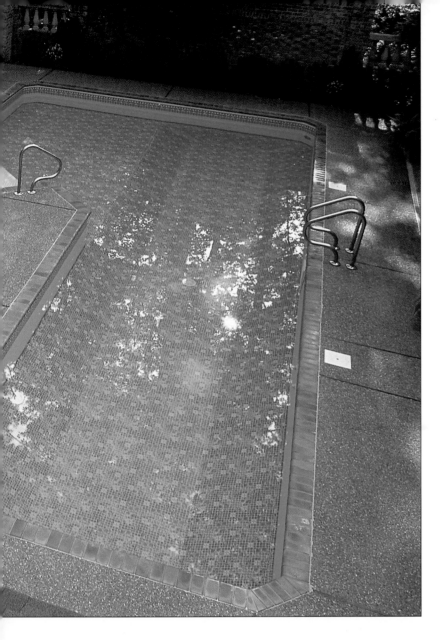

This nicely laid-out, vinyl-lined pool with separate lap-swimming and play areas is much less expensive to construct than its concrete counterpart. This functional yet pretty pool truly illustrates how less can be more: the aggregate pool decking, elegant pool furniture, and subdued landscaping combine to create a sophisticated poolscape.

which are most often produced at the factory and then trucked to the site, can now be produced on-site, much like free-form concrete pools.

Custom Vinyl-Lined Pool ($$$)

This beautiful, custom vinyl-lined pool was constructed to replace a troublesome, deep, old, leaky pool on unstable fill on a hillside lot. The smaller, shallower replacement pool offers both a lap-swimming area for exercise and a shallow water play area, yet has much less water to heat and treat than the previous pool. Less water in the swimming pool means less chemical maintenance for the pool owner.

The pool has many noteworthy features. Its physical layout is ideal, as it allows for simultaneous water play and lap swimming; the shallow area can be roped off with a safety line to keep children from wandering into the lap area and from disrupting adults who are working out. The recessed ladder in the lap area eliminates obstructions during lap swims, and a recessed stairway with two handrails provides assistance to those getting in and out of the shallow end. The aggregate deck provides excellent drainage through a continuous slotted drainage system found on the perimeter of the entire pool deck, and the bull-nosed coping around the perimeter of the pool prevents slippage and adds an aesthetic element to the package. The wooded surroundings offer serenity to the pool environment but may also increase maintenance. This pool truly illustrates just how sophisticated vinyl-lined pools can be.

Cost-cutting measures could include installing less elaborate fencing and eliminating the pool house. Constructing a pool on a hillside lot is an expensive endeavor, due to the challenges of both engineering and construction. Although the wooded lot is a strong visual asset that enhances privacy, it may cause many housekeeping problems.

Large, Custom Vinyl-Lined Pool ($$$$)

This large, custom vinyl-lined pool illustrates how an entire backyard can be turned into an entertainment center with the pool as its focus. The modified L-shaped pool design is very functional; the diving area and shallow water play areas are set far apart, thereby reducing conflicts in activity.

SPECIAL FEATURES

■ The large pool house, complete with kitchenette, bath house, and storage, adds functional elegance.

■ The extensive landscaping increases the beauty of the poolscape.

■ Considerable masonry work was done to construct walls to seating height.

■ Earth mounding was accomplished to elevate structures for better views of the pool and to improve drainage.

■ A stereo sound system is cleverly hidden in landscaping.

■ Underwater, in-wall benches make it possible for swimmers to rest and relax in the water.

■ The diving board and pole sockets for volleyball add to the pool's entertainment value.

The installation of this vinyl-lined pool went hand in hand with the restoration of the backyard, as the earth removed for the pool was used to elevate the pool house and the remainder of the yard.

This unusable backyard with poor drainage was transformed into an aquatic playground with extensive landscaping and many amenities, such as lighting and a hidden stereo system.

In this particular case, the high cost of this pool project was due to the need for total reconstruction and landscaping of the backyard. (If such reconstruction wasn't necessary, this pool would have been ranked in the $$ to $$$ range.) Before the installation of the pool, this backyard was unattractive and unusable because of poor drainage. By reusing the earth removed for the pool installation, money was saved not only by eliminating disposal costs, but by enabling the builder to create elevations around the pool onto which the pool house and play areas were constructed. French drains (an underground drainage system) were also installed in the yard to improve outflow.

Beautiful masonry walls serve two functions in this project: they separate wet pool-deck areas from dry lawn areas, and because they were constructed at seating height, they provide additional lounging surfaces for nonswimmers. The beautiful wrought-iron fence placed on top of a masonry wall improves security and aesthetics as well. Each stone pillar found in the fence is crowned with an attractive light fixture, which makes the pool an appealing spot for entertaining at night.

Other notable features include underwater benches built into the swimming pool walls, and an elaborate sound system hidden in the landscaping. The landscaping consists of

Special fiberglassing techniques were used to renovate this pool ravaged by California earthquakes. The raised deck overlooking a valley sits on a fortified hillside that was engineered specifically to protect the pool from future damage.

low-maintenance plantings located at sufficient distance from the pool, which add beauty without adding more pool maintenance. The concrete deck is practical, for it is spacious enough to accommodate poolside activities, and it is attractive, thanks to the inlaid bricks.

Cost-cutting measures could include reducing the amount of landscaping and some of the masonry work, installing a less expensive fence, and eliminating or modifying the pool house. Because this is such a well-planned comprehensive project, I would recommend cuts only if the owners could not afford all the options. With such a spacious deck, a spa could have been easily incorporated to make this backyard even more functional.

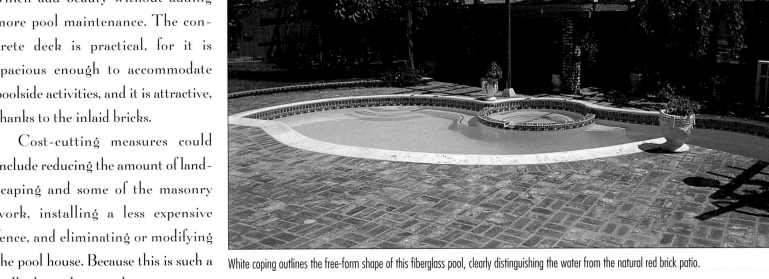

White coping outlines the free-form shape of this fiberglass pool, clearly distinguishing the water from the natural red brick patio.

Free-Form Fiberglass Renovated Pool with Spa ($$$$)

This project is a renovation of an older plaster pool on an unstable hillside lot in California that was severely damaged by earthquakes and a shifting hillside. Much of the effort and cost of this project was spent on fortifying the hillside before restoring the pool. Scores of deep holes were drilled into the bedrock, and considerable amounts of concrete and reinforcing bars were added to prevent the hill from shifting further.

After reinforcements were constructed, the existing pool shell was prepared for a unique three-step fiberglassing process that produces a hard, nonporous finish unaffected by pool water

SPECIAL FEATURES

■ This pool was renovated with a patented fiberglassing technique designed specifically to protect the finish from pool water and chemicals.

■ The hillside on which the pool was built was totally reinforced to protect it from earthquakes and erosion—and cost more than the pool itself.

■ The raised deck behind the pool produces excellent views of both the valley and the pool.

■ The spacious pool deck is attractive and functional.

and chemicals. (This patented process was developed specifically for swimming pools and has been field-tested successfully.) The dark blue accent tiles were placed directly on the fiberglass to prevent them from cracking during earthquakes.

The high wall across from the in-pool spa was built on a high spot on the hillside to create a dramatic view of the valley below as well as offer a bird's-eye view of the pool. A lovely wooden deck was strategically placed between the brick deck and the white wrought-iron fence to conceal the hillside reinforcements and to provide additional space for observing the valley. Other notable features include the in-water step and two love seats that make for easy access in and out of the pool from two sides of the deck as well as from the spa—the edge of each is tiled, marking it for safety. Finally, the bright white coping around the pool provides a nice contrast to the beautiful natural brick deck and adds an element of safety too, thanks to its nonslip surface, while the spacious deck has ample room for poolside activities. The potted plants are attractive and add color, yet are virtually maintenance-free.

Cost-cutting measures could include substituting a less expensive deck material and eliminating the spa. With a little ingenuity, a lap lane for fitness buffs could have been incorporated into the design. A structure to provide more shade than the trellis behind the pool could have been installed as well.

In-Ground Concrete Pools

Generally, concrete pools are more expensive to install than vinyl-lined and fiberglass pools because they require more time, labor, and equipment. But in-ground concrete pools are usually more permanent structures and offer more flexibility in terms of design. Additionally, in-ground pools often increase the value of a home, whereas above-ground pools do not necessarily do so. The price range for concrete pools is quite wide— and costs depend heavily upon geographical location. A concrete pool that costs $20,000 to install in Pennsylvania, for example, may cost only $10,000 in Arizona.

Small, Naturalistic, Kidney-Shaped Pool

($$$) This simple, pretty, and inexpensive pool adds to the natural setting of the backyard of this home while clearly illustrating how many amenities a pool can lack and still remain attractive and functional. This pool was planned more for aesthetics than for swimming and is a nice addition to the garden, thanks to its pondlike landscaping.

The only real amenity in this very basic pool is the set of "wedding-cake" (circular) steps serving the same function in the shallow end. A slide would make the pool more enjoyable for children; a deck would support a variety of poolside activities; and a hot tub or spa would promote relaxation. An interesting focal point is the centrally placed boulder around which the pool appears to be form-fitted. A small deck or spa might work well if fitted between the boulder and the pool. Of course, any addition would likewise increase the cost of the project.

The back side of the pool behind the boulder is well landscaped, bordered by a beautiful stone wall trimmed with colorful flowers. The stone wall matches the coping stones around the pool perfectly. The wall also serves to elevate the pool to a level above the remainder of the backyard.

Although the pool's attractiveness is due in great part to its natural setting, leaves and grass clippings could cause housekeeping problems. Mowing the lawn around this pool may

---

Special Features

■ This is an inexpensive, bare-bones concrete pool; there are no extras.
■ The gray pool bottom matches Long Island Sound in the background, enhancing the pool's natural look, as do the coping stones and boulder.
■ The absence of a pool deck saves money.

This simple and natural pool was built to resemble a natural lake. The pool bottom was painted to match the bay in the background. A deck would have added to the price tag and produced a manufactured look, but the extensive lawn and greenery are sure to make maintenance a chore.

even be a problem because the lawn and pool are so close together.

There are not many cost-cutting measures for this basic yet beautiful pool. Although this is a naturalistic pool, a deck would not only increase poolside activities, but eliminate wear and tear to the lawn area and lessen upkeep. A deck constructed of natural stone, much like what is used in the coping and garden wall, would be attractive. An old-fashioned, redwood hot tub would also work well somewhere on the back side of this swimming pool.

Lake Pool with Waterfall ($$$$)

A wooded lot offers an attractive, naturalistic setting for this pool with a waterfall as its centerpiece. A designer specializing in masonry and landscaping was called in to assist the pool builder in creating the perfect setting for this beautiful and functional free-form gunite "lake" with a dark bottom. Lush landscaping in raised rock gardens grows down to the water's edge, while a bluestone deck greatly enhances the natural look. Literally tons of natural stone were used to construct the waterfalls, coping, and decking.

In addition to the large, "wedding-cake" steps, the pool has a settee built off the second step that provides a relaxing place to sit. The builder handled the required deep-water exit by installing "Hollywood" (built-in) steps rather than the more conventional ladder. Stone "grabs" were used to facilitate leaving the pool and to maintain the very natural look of the poolscape.

While the cost of the pool itself was not inexpensive, the decking, rockscaping, and plantings actually exceeded that of the pool. Note the proliferation of annuals, ornamental grasses,

and trees (Japanese maple, blue spruce, and white birch) showcased at poolside. The landscaping is so natural, one would think the plants had been there all along.

It would be difficult to suggest cost-cutting measures without diminishing the "lake effect" of this pool. Depending on the owners' taste, some decking could be added to the far side of the pool for additional space, but I would not reduce any of the existing deck. A spa could easily be added and would contribute significantly to the versatility of the pool.

SPECIAL FEATURES

■ The waterfall was placed in elevated landscaping at little added expense.

■ The spacious, randomly shaped deck adds beauty and function.

■ The pool uses Westchester stone (granite) coping and a dark, marbleized interior, which enhances the natural look.

■ The pool has large, "wedding-cake" steps, with a built-in settee.

The natural look of this mountain-lake poolscape was created in several ways. The specialized masonry work fits in well with the landscaping, which is rather extensive. The waterfall, requiring tons of natural stone, provides a nice focal point for the project, while the ornamental trees bordering the perimeter of the pool provide contrast. The granite coping stones and bluestone deck complement each other and enhance the natural look of the pool.

Free-Form Pool with Spa ($$$$)

This medium-size naturalistic pool combines several functional elements of good pool design with unique features. The owners, a married couple, did the majority of the work themselves; they installed the deck, the stonework, the waterfalls, and the landscaping, and built the cabana. This ambitious project took the pair nearly three years of hard work to complete, but the finished result is exactly what they wanted in a pool and pool environment.

The unique features and personal touches of this pool are many. The cabana is constructed of old barn rafters made of yellow pine that were sent by barge to the owners' residence. The top of the bar inside the cabana is made of antique brass. The free-form pool deck utilizes Riverside slate, a cast-in-place, colored, textured, and imprinted architectural concrete paving. The pool is self-cleaning—fifteen jets were installed to circulate the water and remove dirt. The concrete spa is perfectly situated: it is readily accessible from both the deck and pool. Beautiful stone and concrete steps connect the house to

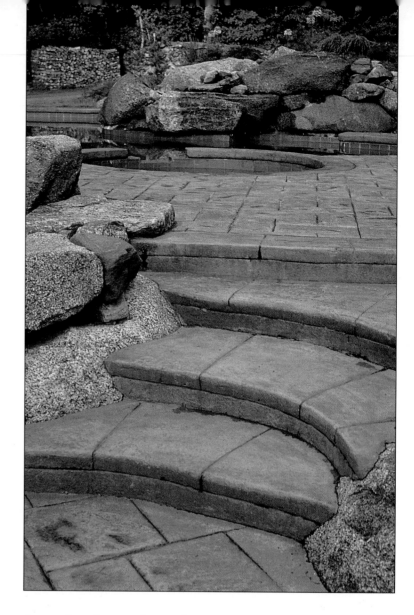

the pool and spa. Those who are interested in a medium-size pool that neither disrupts the natural landscape nor dominates the backyard will appreciate this case study.

Cost-cutting measures could include eliminating the cabana, spa, or waterfalls. Although the cabana is a lovely addition and has many personal touches, some homeowners may prefer a less elaborate and expensive structure. The in-pool spa is perfectly placed, although a raised, rustic hot tub by the waterfalls might be an interesting option. The deck could be expanded on the far side of the pool to increase poolside activities.

SPECIAL FEATURES

■ The pool has a custom-made cabana with a shower and an antique brass bar, which adds elegance and convenience.

■ The pool has waterfalls.

■ The project incorporates profuse landscaping and natural stone outcroppings.

■ The pool is bordered by masonry walls and a custom-imprinted concrete deck—durable, attractive materials that make it easy to keep the pool clean.

Almost every detail of this swimming pool project was done by the homeowners themselves. The pool deck and steps (detail on the opposite page) connecting the pool to the house was a pet project, as was the custom-made cabana.

Formal Lap Pool ($$$) Lap pools are generally less expensive to construct and to maintain than larger, free-form pools. This pool is a fine example of the popular lap pool. It was built by serious swimmers who were not interested in the upkeep required of pool ownership. Consequently, many labor-saving devices were added, including disinfection by a combination of ozone and bromine, rather than chlorine; an in-floor cleaning system; and an automatic safety cover.

The formal, geometric look of this project was achieved in several ways. The pool, patio, house, and landscape are brought together by beautiful bluestone decking. The extensive stonework not only achieves a stately look but also makes

Built for serious swimmers, this no-nonsense lap pool is stately and maintenance-free, and includes many work-saving gadgets. The recessed ladders located at both ends of the pool are an important feature, as they do not create obstruction for lap swimmers.

maintenance easy and minimal. The plantings and patio furniture are placed symmetrically: two nicely landscaped raised stone beds at opposite ends of the patio add interest and color to the long rectangular layout of the pool. Likewise, recessed ladders that do not conflict with lap swimming are found at both ends of the pool. A small lawn and a large flower garden

Stonework reduces maintenance by keeping debris out of the water. The perennial garden on the back of the lot softens the poolscape without increasing maintenance.

are located across from the pool opposite the house, adding color and beauty without adding excessive maintenance.

Cost-cutting measures could include reducing the scope of the stonework and eliminating some of the automation, but a real cost-saver would be to eliminate the deep end, which requires a great deal of water without significantly adding to the function of the lap pool. A spa or hot tub could easily be added for relaxation and therapy after workouts. Likewise, a cabana could be added for versatility and shade. A shorter lap pool of this type might work almost as well on a smaller lot if sufficient room was not available for a pool this large.

Lap Pool Plus ($$$)

This gym and swim lap pool is extremely versatile: it provides lap swimming for adults, shallow-water play areas for children, and an attractive setting for relaxing and entertaining, thanks to its fountains and dramatic lighting. The pool's design is well thought out, as serious lap swimming and other water activities can occur at once.

In addition to being the same length (75 feet [22.9m]) as competitive swimming pools, this pool has several creative features. Fiber-optic lighting and plate-glass block were installed on the pool walls at water level to produce a dramatic visual effect, particularly at night. Three telescopic fountains built into the floor transform the pool into a beautiful site perfect for entertaining at the push of a button. Because this pool is so long, two automatic vacuums were installed at each end to clean the pool properly.

In addition, an abundance of landscaping surrounds the pretty and functional pool deck, constructed of epoxy stone coating over concrete and linked to the pool with brick coping. The strong exterior fencing provides both security and privacy.

Cost-cutting measures could include eliminating the fiber-optic lighting, fountains, or plate-glass block, which add ambience and aesthetics but not function. On a smaller lot, this same pool could be shortened to 60 feet (18m) and still function effectively as a lap pool. For larger families, the play areas in the pool could be expanded slightly. The deck could also be expanded to increase poolside activities.

SPECIAL FEATURES

■ This is a full-length, 75-foot (22.9m) lap pool that has play areas and offers an attractive setting for entertaining.

■ Fiber-optic lighting and plate-glass block have been installed on the pool walls for dramatic visual effect.

■ Three telescopic fountains have been built into the floor of the pool.

■ Two automatic vacuums make it possible to clean opposite ends of the pool simultaneously.

Although this lap pool is competition length, its unusual shape, deck, fountains, and lighting make it suitable for relaxing and entertaining.

Large, Free-Form Pool with Bridge and Spa($$$)

This pool contains numerous unique features as well as many work-saving and cost-cutting gadgets. The owners of this home added a randomly shaped pool to give the impression of having three pools in one and to connect the backyard to the tennis court and guest house. The principal function of this swimming pool is to entertain, as evidenced by the elaborate decking and wealth of pool furniture.

Of special interest is the bridge, which serves to link the home to the tennis court and guest house, adding both access and aesthetics to the project, although it could add slightly to upkeep. A raised spa with a waterfall that overlooks the pool and bridge adds another practical yet attractive element to the project. The deck is spacious, offering room for poolside activities, and visually interesting, as combinations of wood, concrete, and brick are all used tastefully. The clusters of pool furniture are not overdone and add usability to the deck.

But perhaps the most intriguing aspect of the pool is what you can't see—computerized maintenance. Lights, heaters, disinfection, waterfalls, and numerous other features are controlled automatically. The pool also has an automatic in-floor cleaning system.

Cost-cutting measures could include eliminating the bridge, raised spa, and/or computerization. For those interested in fitness, a less random pool design might encourage lap swimming.

This pretty pool connects the home to a guest house and tennis courts and is fully automated. The bridge and raised spa create two separate focal points for the project.

SPECIAL FEATURES

■ There is elaborate decking and pool furniture that enhances the pool's beauty and function.

■ The bridge over the pool provides beauty as well as access to other parts of the yard.

■ The raised spa provides a bird's-eye view of the pool.

■ The waterfall flowing from spa to pool adds a nice aesthetic touch.

■ The in-floor cleaning system saves a lot of work.

■ A computerized system makes maintenance virtually effortless.

■ The filtration equipment is hidden in an artificial boulder.

This complete pool project seems to provide many small pools in one without overwhelming the backyard. The spacious deck allows for ample landscaping and pool furniture without overcrowding.

Large Lagoon ($$$$) This creative pool design demonstrates how any yard can be retrofitted to accommodate a beautiful pool. The owner of this pool was afraid of losing too much of his lovely, lush backyard lawn. To preserve the lawn, the pool builder constructed a long, narrow lagoon on the back of the lot.

Of special interest are the thousands of boulders used to construct the walls, waterfalls, walks, and decks. Tanning stones were also strategically placed between the pool and the spa above. In fact, all of the steps are carefully placed stones that link different elements of the project together.

The result is a pool that looks natural rather than constructed. Lush tropical plants, including many different species of ferns and vines, are planted between stones and grow down to the water's edge. Because the pool was constructed on a hillside lot, the builders took advantage of the topography and hid

SPECIAL FEATURES

■ Thousands of boulders have been stacked perfectly to create stepping-stones in and out of the pool and spa, and to provide tanning and lounging areas.

■ The five waterfalls and raised spa are well placed, enhancing the pool's natural look.

■ The matching stone deck reduces upkeep and complements the pool's stonework.

■ The filtration equipment is hidden over the embankment.

■ The pool is operated by remote control.

the filtration equipment over the embankment behind the pool. Although the lawn was saved in this case, a portion of it could have been removed to create deck space.

Cost-cutting measures could include minimizing the stonework, eliminating the spa, and hiding the filtration equipment in the boulders near the pool. Eliminating part of the lawn may reduce pool maintenance costs as well. A gazebo or bridge would add interest and versatility to this project.

An oasis in the backyard, this project relied on the perfect placement of boulders to create waterfalls as well as areas for sitting, stepping, and reclining. This pool was constructed with a vertical emphasis in order to preserve the lawn.

Beach Entry ($$$$) This customized pool illustrates the painstaking measures some homeowners and builders will take to produce a pool that perfectly reflects their special interests. In this case, extraordinary effort was taken to produce a natural bush pool for homeowners living in a secluded suburb adjacent to park land in Sydney, Australia. This pool resembles a tropical oasis more than a swimming pool.

One of the functional highlights of this pool is the ease of entry provided by the roll-over coping (a hard, textured, non-slip surface that simulates hard sand) in conjunction with the graded pebble "beach." Ample area for entertainment is also provided along one side of the pool, framed by planters and bush land.

To heighten the natural effect, the entire yard was heavily landscaped with native trees and shrubs. Even the fence was constructed of used native timber. A spa is discreetly tucked under a ferny bank that crowns a waterfall outside the pool, which sends water tumbling into a pond outside the back door.

Chlorine generation from salt is used to disinfect the pool, and a solar heating system maintains the water temperature. The pool also has a full in-floor water circulation and cleaning system.

Cost-cutting measures could include eliminating the waterfall and spa, but this would probably ruin the project aesthetically. A bridge or gazebo might also enhance this project, allowing friends and family to better observe the pool, particularly as profuse plantings encroach the already limited deck space.

SPECIAL FEATURES

- ■ The pool interior is constructed of river pebble that creates a natural-looking and nonslip surface.
- ■ A raised spa is discreetly placed in a ferny bank to ensure privacy.
- ■ Striking waterfalls add to the pool's natural look.
- ■ There is a large, beautiful "beach" area for sunning and ease of entry.
- ■ The pool has an in-floor cleaning system.
- ■ The poolscape contains trees and shrubs native to the Australian bush.

The efforts to make this secluded residential pool resemble a natural pool were enhanced by the installation of simulated pebble beaches and pool bottom. A waterfall hidden in a bank of ferns offers a place for private relaxation.

This Australian Bush pool is naturalistic down to the last detail. Note how the roll-over coping simulates hard sand quite convincingly.

This absolutely spare vanishing-edge lap pool is surrounded by masonry rather than plants to reduce maintenance. The raised spa is strategically placed to overlook both the pool and the valley beyond. The wide recessed steps provide easy access and an area for in-water lounging.

Geometric, Vanishing-Edge Pool ($$$$)

The vanishing-edge pool is a relatively new and quite popular design that works to visually combine the far edge of the pool with the view beyond.

In this case, the pool water seems to disappear into the valley below. This vanishing-edge pool is dramatic but functional, as it includes a raised spa, a spacious deck, and a racing lane for lap swimming. This pool is a clean, maintenance-free choice for serious swimmers.

The owners of this pool chose to keep the poolscape spare so as not to interfere with the view beyond. The spacious deck keeps pool maintenance to a minimum and makes poolside entertaining easy. The absence of landscaping also lessens upkeep considerably. The wide steps not only provide superior access into and out of the pool but also allow room for lounging at the shallow end.

Cost-cutting measures could include substituting a recessed ladder for the steps, which were expensive to construct, and/or eliminating the spa. Plants would add color and variety to the pool deck, which is spacious yet sparse. Shade areas could also be created with umbrellas, awnings, or arbors.

SPECIAL FEATURES

■ The pool has a spectacular vanishing edge, while the raised spa overlooks the valley and pool.

■ The pool features an area for lap swimming.

■ Wide steps make for easy access.

■ The large, spacious, aggregate deck facilitates poolside activities and also helps to keep the pool clean by keeping debris at a distance from the water.

SUPER POOLS

These last two case studies are best described as super pools, as both were planned as centerpieces for entertainment, and cost was not a factor. Because the pools were meticulously built without constraints to fulfill the wishes of the homeowners, it would be presumptuous to offer suggestions. Both pools are formal, and the style of each relied upon the architecture of the house and lifestyle of the owners. For these reasons, cost-cutting measures and options will not be discussed, either. Pools such as these require a great deal of engineering and contain many custom-made features (such as hand-cut tile), so costs are enormous. Super pools usually start at about $100,000 and can easily run into the millions.

Formal Dreamscape ($$$$$)
This spectacular contemporary Mediterranean pool system closely resembles a Roman bath, and the surrounding yard produces an amphitheaterlike effect. This elegant pool sits below the house and overlooks a valley, which creates a dramatic view. There is limited landscaping on the deck level. Most plantings are found in containers, including the trees that are the focus of the project: this helps keep maintenance down and adds elegance overall. The view from the pool and the large, lush lawn add color and interest to the arid backdrop.

The large, spacious deck incorporates a variety of different-colored stones, offers ample room for entertainment, and makes it easy to keep the pool clean. A sunken bar at poolside offers seating for spectators and swimmers, and a large barbecue pit enhances social functions. The project also features extensive lighting, which can be found in the water, in the landscaping, and on all permanent structures.

The pool itself has many wonderful features. There are lovely walk-in entries on opposite ends of the pool, while in-water benches run its entire length. Large spillways on the far side of the pool provide a beautiful view from the house, and the sound of the falling water functions at poolside to keep conversation private. The custom-shaped spa overflows into the pool as well. All pool functions are totally automated.

SPECIAL FEATURES

- The spillways on the far side of the pool provide beauty and privacy.
- Spacious walk-in entries are provided on opposite ends of the pool.
- A sunken bar with both "wet" and "dry" seating arrangements enables swimmers to chat with spectators.
- Remote-controlled pool operations make upkeep easy.
- The pool has outstanding panoramic views.

Ideal for entertainment, this comprehensive pool project is obviously the centerpiece of this home, for it contains many extra amenities such as walk-in entries, wet and dry seating, a bar, and an irregularly shaped spa. Outstanding views are also enhanced by the pool setting; the home overlooks the pool, and the pool in turn overlooks the mountains.

Saltwater Pool and Spa ($$$$$)

This traditional, award-winning pool project was selected not only for its grandeur but because it is a saltwater rather than a freshwater pool (saltwater is better for the skin and creates greater buoyancy). This pool incorporates specially hand-cut coral flagstones to match the house perfectly. The classic radius ends of the pool are lightened with raised flagstone accents. Note the minimal landscaping in this project.

The formal white arbor and fencing add distinction and a reprieve from the sun. Of particular interest are the stone columns found in the arbor. The columns conceal a stereo system, and there are speakers underwater as well.

The fully automated, raised spa overlooking the pool has a unique, removable, cascading fountain. The spa also offers multilevel seating and all-tile arm rests. As an added touch, spa water overflows down a spillway into the pool. In-water bar stools can be found in the pool opposite the spa, while a long reclining stone bench is built into the decking.

The poolside bar of this French Mediterranean saltwater pool and spa is the ultimate in luxury, with stools located in the water, a beautiful tile countertop, and coral deck coping.

SPECIAL FEATURES

■ This pool has in-pool bar stools and a custom-made 30-foot (10m) reclining bench.

■ The raised spa has a removable fountain.

■ The stone conceals stereo speakers.

■ Pool disinfection is provided by chlorine generation through salt water.

■ This pool and spa is self-cleaning and all of its functions are computerized.

This saltwater pool and spa with a removable fountain features classic radius ends and raised coral flagstone and coral accents. The stone columns house a sound system, and there are underwater speakers as well.

Part II

CARE AND MAINTENANCE

Chapter Five

Circulation, Chemistry, and Maintenance

There's no way around it. Swimming pools can require a lot of mechanical and chemical attention. But if you know what you're doing, operating a safe, clean, and enjoyable pool can be quite easy. To simplify pool operations, the pool must be outfitted with the right equipment and chemicals. Even if you contract with a swimming pool service company to take care of all your pool maintenance, you must have a basic understanding of the swimming pool system. Understanding the basics will save you time and money, as you won't be calling the dealer as often to correct simple pool problems.

Circulation, filtration, and chemistry are three concepts that are vital to understanding the successful functioning of a swimming pool system. Proper water chemistry, filtration, and good circulation go hand in hand to produce clean, clear water.

To understand the importance of any pool circulation system, you must first understand the concepts of water clarity and water quality. Basically, water clarity refers to the visibility of the water. Water quality refers to the amount of bacteria and other harmful organisms in the pool. Water with good clarity is transparent and enables all underwater features of the pool shell to be clearly visible. It is possible, however, for water to have good water clarity and poor water quality. There are a lot of pretty, clear pools that contain contaminated water.

Chemical disinfectants are added to pools to ensure good water quality, but

Tropical trees and flowers provide a beautiful backdrop for this pretty, free-form pool and spa combination. The perimeter walls provide privacy and security without obstructing a view of the mountains.

proper pool filtration is the first step in achieving good water. Outstanding water chemistry cannot make up for inadequate filtration and vice versa.

■ ■ ■

THE CIRCULATION SYSTEM

To keep the water clear and clean, a swimming pool comes equipped with a circulation system. The circulation system is often referred to as the pool's support system. The main purposes of the circulation system are to remove dirt and debris by filtering the water and to aid in the distribution of disinfecting chemicals. For the circulation system to be effective, there must be water moving through it continually.

The circulation system of a pool or spa is analogous to the circulation system in the human body. Pool water, just like blood in the human body, is constantly moving in a loop. A pool pump pushes the pool water through the system in the same way that the heart pushes blood. The pool filter reduces contaminants just as our kidneys do.

The most important components of the circulation system are the pool outlets, the pool inlets, the hair and lint strainer, the pool pump, and the filters—this chapter will go into these components in detail. The heater, the chemical feeders, and the gauges, valves, and meters are also important, but maintenance and problem solving in these

areas should be left to experts, and will therefore not be covered here.

Pool Outlets
In the pool circulation system, water leaves the pool through outlets to return to the pool pump. There are two types of pool outlets, and both are required for adequate circulation. The first is the surface skimmer, which is located along the pool wall on the surface; the second is the main drain, which is found at the deepest point in the pool. The main drain is also used to empty the pool when necessary.

Surface skimmers are one of the most important components of the circulation system. Most swimming pool contaminants (dirt, pollen, leaves, and oil) enter the pool on the water surface, and the surface skimmer is designed to pull debris from the surface before it has a chance to sink to the bottom. To ensure good surface skimming action, there should be one skimmer for every 500 square feet (46.5 sq m) of surface area. At least one skimmer should be placed on the downwind side of your pool. (See also page 60 in chapter two.)

Within the recessed box that makes up the skimmer is a basket that catches large debris such as leaves. This skimmer basket must be cleaned manually and checked daily to guarantee good skimming and filtering. Skimmers also have a regulating gate, or weir, that ensures good skimming action. Children must be prevented from playing

This pool house is perfectly situated, as it overlooks the pool and spa and is within earshot of the fountain.

with the gates so that their hands or feet don't become trapped in them. Skimmer covers located on the deck must be nonslip. Skimmers with chemical feeders are available, as are float valves that can be placed in the skimmer and that automatically add water when the pool level is low.

Gutters provide a continuous trough around the surface of the pool and produce outstanding surface skimming action, but they are used most often at large public pools and will not be discussed here.

The main drain outlet on the pool bottom also works to return water to the filters. When the pool bottom is littered with leaves or other debris, the valves can be adjusted to pull more water through the main drain to help clean the bottom. When brushing the pool, it is helpful to increase the suction from the main drain.

The main drain must have antivortex plates or covers in place to dissipate suction. The drain cover should be a tamperproof, corrosion-resistant grate in a color that contrasts with the bottom of the pool. The slots in the grates must not be wider than a half inch (12.7mm) to prevent entrapment. It is preferable that pools have more than one drain, and all drains should have antivortex plates.

Pool Inlets

Inlets return filtered, heated, and chemically treated water back to the pool. Inlets provide those surprisingly strong jets of water that tickle you as you hold on to the side of the pool. Inlets are most often located on pool walls, although in some pools they are located on the bottom. It is imperative that pool inlets be placed strategically so that chemicals are distributed evenly throughout the pool. Improper placement of inlets can create dead spots (see also page 60 in chapter two), which are difficult to detect. Algae growth in certain areas is a telltale sign of this circulation inadequacy. Adjustable inlets can be purchased that enable you to direct the treated water to the exact spots where it is needed most.

The Hair and Lint Strainer

The pool pump must be protected by a strainer pot that collects hair, lint, bobby pins, leaves, and other foreign bodies. This strainer, located near the pool pump, protects your pool pump from damage and should be checked daily; otherwise, you may end up with a clogged strainer that impairs the flow of water through the filters and causes cloudy water. Checking the strainer pot and skimmer baskets is the best way to guarantee proper filtering flow rates. The lid on the strainer must always be tightly secured or air will be drawn into the pump and pushed back into the pool. This is not good, as air in the system can damage the pump or turn the pool cloudy.

The Pool Pump

The pump is the center of every pool's circulation system. Centrifugal pumps are used in the pool industry. These pumps are simple, reliable devices that use centrifugal force to throw out water through impeller blades. The key to selecting any pool pump is to match its pumping capacity with the volume of your pool. An undersized pump will not produce sufficient turnovers (a turnover takes place when the entire volume of water in the pool passes through the filtration system) to filter the water properly, whereas an oversized pump may damage other pool parts by pushing pool water too forcefully through small openings.

Most swimming pools require a turnover every six to eight hours (three to four turns a day). While in use, hot tubs and spas require a turnover every thirty minutes. Selecting the appropriate pump to maintain proper filtration is essential. Pool professionals use standard pump curves to determine the best pump for a given pool. The pool dealer should share this important information with you.

The Filters

Just as the pump is the heart of the pool circulation system, the filters are its kidneys. As the pool water is circulated, it is passed through a filter or bank of filters where dirt, hair, pollen, and other small particles are trapped and, when the filter media is cleaned, flushed out of the system. In most cases, pool water enters the top of the filter tank, travels downward through the filter medium, and exits as clean water at the bottom of the filter tank.

It is important to note that the filters do not remove bacteria, viruses, fungi, or algae. Killing bacteria and other harmful organisms is the job of the disinfection system. Although adequate turnovers are an important prerequisite for good water clarity, the type of filter medium has much to do with the effectiveness of the filter. Basically, there are three types of filter media: sand, diatomaceous earth (DE), and cartridge. Filters that produce the best water clarity may also require the most work. Before deciding on a particular filter, weigh the importance of superior water clarity against ease of operation. (Because I am very particular about water clarity, I favor DE filtration.) Overall, the cost of these filters is similar, and they all should be cleaned weekly.

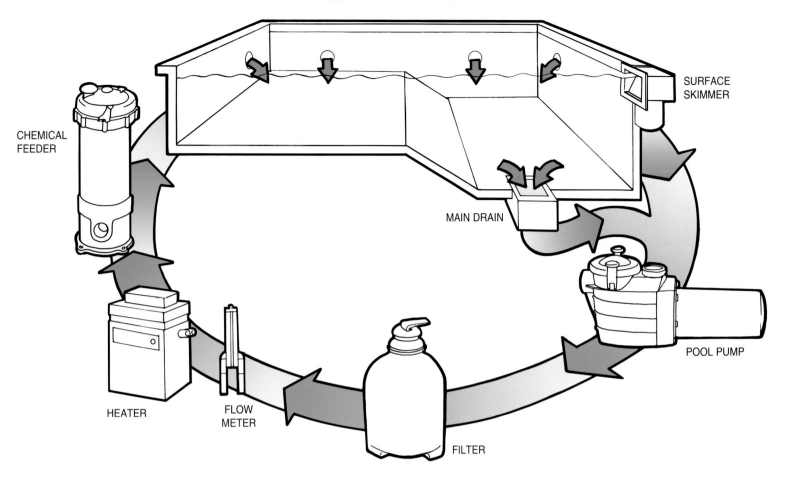

This flow chart illustrates the basics of pool-water circulation. Pool water constantly leaves the pool through bottom and surface outlets, is pushed through a pool filter for cleaning, is heated and chemically treated, and is again evenly distributed throughout the pool.

CHEMICAL FEEDER

SURFACE SKIMMER

MAIN DRAIN

POOL PUMP

HEATER

FLOW METER

FILTER

Sand Filtration Sand is perhaps the most popular filter medium. Sand is a perpetual filtration medium that rarely needs replacing, a feature that you may find attractive. Sand filters are exceptionally easy to maintain and operate; they also work well in most pool applications. One drawback of sand filters, though, is that they can allow finer particles to pass through the circulation system. Most sand filters can trap dirt particles that are 25 micrometers in size and larger. (Particles that are 35 micrometers or larger are visible to the naked eye; a grain of common table salt is about 90 micrometers

and human hair is 70 micrometers.) By comparison, DE filters can screen out particles that are approximately 3 micrometers in size, and cartridge filters can trap dirt that is 5 to 10 micrometers.

Backwashing is the term used to describe the cleaning of the sand system, and it refers to the reversal of the flow of water in order to push the accumulated dirt in the filter tank out to waste. Most residential pools use high-rate sand filtration, which utilizes the entire depth of the sand to trap dirt. DE and cartridge filters utilize only the surface of the medium to collect dirt.

Diatomaceous Earth Filtration Diatomaceous earth (DE) filters employ the fossilized skeletal remains of marine life, sometimes referred to as diatoms, to clean the pool. Each diatom is 90 percent air space and 10 percent fossil. The irregular shapes of the air molecules, combined with pores and crevices in the DE, enable this substance to trap a great deal of dirt, just like a sponge. As a result, DE filters consistently produce clear, sparkling water.

DE does have disadvantages, however. Unlike sand, DE is a temporary medium, meaning that it must be replaced. When a conventional DE filter is cleaned, you must dispose of the dirty DE. New DE must then be placed on the filter septa (the screen that holds the DE). When handling DE, it is very important to wear a protective mask to prevent inhalation of the powder, as DE can be a lung irritant. DE filter systems have been vastly improved in recent years, however. Regenerative DE filters now allow you to "bump" the filter: bumping is a process that allows the DE to realign itself on the filter septa, enabling it to catch additional dirt. Regenerative DE filters can have long filter cycles by reusing the same DE to filter dirt. As a result, regenerative DE filters don't have to be changed nearly as often as conventional DE systems. The DE in a regenerative system may be changed a couple of times each season. The DE in a conventional system will probably be changed once a week.

Most pool owners dispose of used DE as household trash. But in some areas, the used DE must be separated out from the used pool water, bagged, then placed in a special waste disposal system.

Cartridge Filtration

Cartridge filtration is a relatively new filtration system. Pool cartridge filters are similar to air filters that protect automobile carburetors. The cartridge system employs a pleated polyester cloth or other synthetic fabric to trap pool dirt. As the pores of the fabric become clogged with dirt, the cartridge needs to be cleaned or replaced. These filters produce excellent water clarity, as they screen out particles 10 microns and larger.

There are several other advantages to the cartridge filter. Cartridge filtration saves significant amounts of water because the filters are cleaned by hand and not backwashed (which wastes water) like other pressure filters. Cartridge filter systems are also very simple to disassemble, analyze, repair, and replace, and most cartridge filtration systems do not even require tools. Cartridge filters require little space, and use fewer valves and plumbing than do more traditional filtration systems.

Cartridge filtration has disadvantages, too. Some people complain that cartridge filters are difficult to clean and that new filters are required often. Those who use cartridge filters often have new ones on hand to replace old filters every year or so. The plastic lids, O-rings, and gaskets must be checked and lubricated regularly. The lids should be replaced periodically because the plastic lid covers that hold the cartridges in place have been known to crack.

Cartridge filtration appears to be more popular with spas and hot tubs than with pools, although small residential pools can make good use of this system. Most successful cartridge systems use two sets of cartridge filters: one is used in the filter while the other is being soaked in detergent for its next turn in the filter.

Armed with this information, you should have enough facts and figures to make educated decisions about effective circulation equipment. Remember, this is not an area in which you should cut costs: buy a top-of-the-line filter. Most pool problems can be avoided with a good filter, although nothing can correct poor disinfection. Make it a point to understand the components of the circulation system and you're on your way to having a trouble-free pool.

■ ■ ■

WATER CHEMISTRY

Like good circulation, chemical treatment is vital to having clean, clear, and bacteria-free pool and spa water. The chemical disinfectant used in swimming pools provides two important distinct functions: disinfection and oxidation.

Disinfection is the process of destroying microorganisms and bacteria. More specifically, disinfection refers to the destruction of bacteria, viruses, algae, and other pathogens in order to prevent the transmission of disease and other swimmer discomforts such as burning eyes and itching skin. To provide efficient and continuous bacteria control, the pool disinfectant must have residual properties.

Oxidation refers to the breaking down of organic debris. Chemical oxidation assists filtration by decreasing the amount of debris

Much more than a wall, this poolside barrier provides the base for a unique spillway into the pool and for plant life. Spillways and waterfalls have become quite popular because they are attractive and functional.

the filters must handle. Killing bacteria is a relatively easy task for pool chemicals; even small amounts of chlorine will destroy most pathogens. When the swimmer load is high, correspondingly higher levels of chlorine are necessary to rid the pool of the additional organic debris.

Pool practitioners often say "chlorine burns the trash and the filters remove the ash." This simple statement may help you to understand the important relationship between chemistry and filtration. You may blame dull-looking pool water on poor filtration, when in reality, insufficient oxidation due to a lack of pool chemicals is the real culprit.

POPULAR DISINFECTANTS: CHLORINE AND BROMINE

Before selecting a pool disinfectant, make sure you understand what it can and cannot do for you. The following information will help you to make wise choices when it comes to selecting pool chemicals.

Although there are numerous swimming pool disinfectants, chlorine is still the chemical of choice for many pool owners. Chlorine disinfection has been used successfully throughout the world for the treatment of drinking water and is popular for swim-

ming pool use (you may even have more chlorine in the water you drink than in the water in your pool) because it disinfects and oxidizes simultaneously. Not all chemicals accomplish that. Because some people believe that chlorine is the cause of eye irritation and itching skin (it is not: chloramines and unbalanced water cause these problems), there has been an increased interest in using chlorine alternatives. Although numerous pool disinfectants are available, many of them do not provide oxidation, so more chemicals are necessary when using them.

Types of Chlorine
Chlorine is available in three basic forms: gas, liquid, and solid. Although gas chlorine is the most effective and inexpensive type of chlorine, it is also extremely toxic and can even be lethal. For the most part, gas chlorine is not allowed in residential pools; it is mainly used in commercial and public pools. Therefore, this chapter will discuss chlorine in its liquid and solid forms only. These traditional forms of chlorine are unstable, that is, they dissipate quickly in sunlight, although there are some newer forms of chlorine that are stabilized. The stabilized chlorines will be discussed later in this chapter.

Perhaps the greatest disadvantage of chlorine is the production of combined chlorine in pools. When free available chlorine

Chemical Safety

Swimming Pool Oxidizers

Calcium Hypochlorite   Lithium Hypochlorite
Sodium Hypochlorite   Trichlor
Sodium Dichlor   Potassium Peroxymonosulfate

Protective Equipment
- Eyes: goggles
- Hands: gloves (rubber, neoprene, or PVC)
- Body: coveralls and rubber boots
- Lungs: chlorine gas/dust mask. Provide ventilation where dust is likely

Handling Precautions
- Do not take internally
- Avoid contact with eyes, skin, or clothing
- Upon contact with skin or eyes, rinse with water
- Avoid breathing dust
- Store all containers in a cool, dry place
- Do not store containers in direct sunlight
- Do not store near combustible materials
- Do not mix oxidizers
- Use clean, dry utensils when handling oxidizers
- Keep all oxidizer containers off wet floors
- Do not mix oxidizers with anything but water. Always add chemicals to plenty of cool water, never the reverse

Conditions and Materials to Avoid
- Excessive heat. Oxidizers will decompose, releasing toxic gases and heat
- Solvents
- Acids
- Other pool chemicals such as algicides, clarifiers, sequestering agents, and surface cleaners
- Organic materials

Swimming Pool Acids

Muriatic Acid (Hydrochloric Acid, Dilute)   Sodium Bisulfate

Protective Equipment
- Eyes: goggles or full face shield as splashing may occur
- Hands: gloves (rubber, neoprene, or PVC)
- Body: coveralls and rubber boots
- Lungs: chlorine gas/dust respirator

Handling Precautions
- Do not take internally
- Avoid contact with eyes, skin, or clothing
- Upon contact with skin or eyes, rinse with water
- Avoid breathing vapors (muriatic acid) and dust (sodium bisulfate)
- Store all containers in a cool, dry place
- Always add acid to plenty of cool water, never the reverse

Conditions and Materials to Avoid
- Avoid contact with strong alkalies such as caustic soda and sodium carbonate
- Avoid contact with all oxidizers
- Do not store in wet or moist conditions
- Do not store in direct sunlight

Balance Chemicals

Sodium Bicarbonate   Sodium Sesquicarbonate
Sodium Carbonate   Sodium Hydroxide
Calcium Chloride-Dihydrate

Protective Equipment
- Eyes: goggles
- Hands: gloves (rubber, neoprene, or PVC)
- Body: impervious boots (rubber)
- Lungs: gas/dust mask or respirator

Handling Precautions
- Do not take internally
- Avoid contact with eyes, skin, or clothing
- Avoid breathing dust, spray, or mist
- Store all containers in a cool, dry place
- Always keep containers closed
- Caution: considerable heat is generated when sodium hydroxide or calcium chloride-dihydrate is dissolved in water. Use extreme care. Use lukewarm water. Never add to cold or hot water

Conditions and Materials to Avoid
- Avoid contact with acids
- Avoid contact with small volumes of water
- Do not store near acids

Chlorine Alternatives: A Summary

Type	Advantages	Disadvantages
Bromine	More stable than chlorine at higher temperatures. Bromamines more effective than chloramines.	More expensive. Cannot be stabilized. Can create odors. Can turn water green.
Ozone	Does not require shocking. Reduces amount of pool chemicals used. No eye or skin irritation. Does not affect water balance.	No lasting residual. Can create odors. An additional pool disinfectant must be used. Can be corrosive to equipment.
Ionization	Reduces amount of pool chemicals used. Does not affect balance. No eye or skin irritation.	No lasting residual. Electrodes may be replaced often. Can cause staining. Pool disinfectant must be added.
Ultraviolet light and hydrogen peroxide	Reduce dependency on pool chemicals.	No lasting residual. Difficult to handle and store. More expensive.
Polymeric biquanide	Chlorine-free. Lasts longer than chlorines. Does not bleach or burn.	Expensive. Incompatible with other pool chemicals. May promote algae growth, clog filters, and turn water slightly green.

(FAC) combines with nitrogenous organic wastes that swimmers naturally bring into the pool (perspiration, oil, and so on), the result is obnoxious odors. This compound is called combined available chlorine (CAC) and can only be destroyed by high additional doses of chlorine.

It is important to understand that the chlorine you think you smell is not chlorine. When foul-smelling swimming pool odors reach your nose, the problem is that there is actually an insufficient amount of chlorine in the water—not too much. When pool water begins to burn, irritate, and smell, it's time to replace bad chlorine with lots of good chlorine.

That said, it's important to check your pool water daily for three different chlorine components. The first of the three components is free available chlorine (FAC), or simply free chlorine, the active chlorine that disinfects and oxidizes the pool, keeping it safe and comfortable for you and your guests. Free chlorine is "good" chlorine. But as more people enter your pool, free chlorine combines with natural body by-products to create chloramines or "bad chlorine." This makes for the second component of chlorine, combined available chlorine (CAC). CAC is a major pool problem and can take much of the joy out of swimming.

Ironically, in order to purge the pool of chloramines, ten times the amount of combined chlorine must be added to the pool in free chlorine. Most test kits explain how to do this. For instance, if the FAC reading is 1.0 ppm or mgl, and the total available chlorine (TAC), the third component of chlorine, reading is 3.0 ppm/mgl, then 20 ppm/mgl of free chlorine must be added to rid the pool of 2.0 ppm/mgl (CAC) (TAC - FAC = CAC × 10 ppm/mgl). This required remedy is called shocking, or superchlorination, and requires that you either close your pool temporarily until the free chlorine drops to an acceptable level or use nonchlorine shocking agents that are now becoming quite popular.

Calcium Hypochlorite Calcium hypochlorite, or Cal Hypo as it is sometimes called, is a dry form of chlorine that is available in both granular and tablet form. Calcium hypochlorite is 65 percent available chlorine, has a long shelf life, and is easily stored. A cool, dark storage place and a tightly secured lid will go a long way in extending its life.

In residential pools, calcium hypochlorite tablets are placed in erosion feeders or surface skimmers, where they are dissolved and disseminated throughout the pool. In some cases, you may use granular or powdered chlorine, but it is best to dissolve it in water before distributing it into the pool. Many people keep granular calcium hypochlorite on hand for a variety of pool-keeping chores, as it kills algae on contact and is useful in dissolving stains.

One disadvantage of calcium hypochlorite is that it is extremely flammable. Just about any organic material added to this type of chlorine will cause combustion. In fact, soda, oil, sweat, paper, soap, other chemicals, and almost anything else will cause a fire when mixed with calcium hypochlorite. For these reasons, it is imperative that you store calcium hypochlorite separately to prevent other chemicals and organic substances from accidentally mixing with it. The drums in which it is stored must be kept off the floor, and separate chemical scoops and buckets must be used when applying it.

Calcium hypochlorite is unstable, dissipating quickly in sunlight, although it can be stabilized with cyanuric acid to extend its life in the sun.

Sodium Hypochlorite Sodium hypochlorite is a liquid form of chlorine that is 12–15 percent available chlorine and is often referred to as liquid chlorine or just bleach. Sodium hypochlorite is similar to household bleach, but over-the-counter bleach should not be used as a primary sanitizer in your swimming pool. Household bleach is only 5–6 percent active chlorine, and, because of all the inert material in bleach, can clog the filter media. You can use household bleach only to tide you over until you can get to your pool supply store for the real stuff. Perhaps the greatest advantage of

Instant Fireworks

Calcium hypochlorite in tablet form must be placed in an open erosion feeder, never in a closed or pressure feeder intended for trichlor tablets or in a brominator. Many swimming installations that once used calcium hypochlorite in open erosion feeders have upgraded to trichlor or bromine, both of which require special feeders. It is not an uncommon mistake for someone around a pool to place old sodium hypochlorite tablets in a trichlor or bromine feeder. When calcium hypchlorite is dissolved by water under pressure, excessive heat and gases become trapped in the feeder because there is nowhere for them to escape to, and as a result, a fire or explosion can result. A new lifeguard made this very mistake at a hotel in my area and blew up the entire filter room. Another new lifeguard thought he would save a trip to the pool by combining algicide and calcium hypochlorite in the same bucket. Fortunately, he dropped the bucket because it became too hot to handle. He didn't get hurt, but the dramatic fireball he produced taught him a valuable lesson about chemical safety.

Right: Because of its size, this waterfall has a rippling effect on the pool water, increasing the natural look of the pool and causing light to dance across the surface.

sodium hypochlorite is that it is easy and safe to handle and store. The major disadvantage is that it has a short shelf life and is very unstable, so its disinfectant properties diminish quickly in sunlight and at high temperatures.

Sodium hypochlorite also significantly increases the pH of the water. When sodium hypochlorite is used, it must be counterbalanced by a strong acid like sodium bisulfate or muriatic acid to keep the pH within the ideal range. When handling sodium hypochlorite and acids, be certain to wear gloves and a face shield for protection. Sodium hypochlorite is introduced to the pool by a chemical feeder (pump). Chemical feeders tend to clog often, so it's important to clean the feeder regularly. Lithium

hypochlorite is another powdered chlorine, but it is used so infrequently that it will not be discussed here.

Stabilized Chlorines

If you are unable to keep chlorine in your pool on sunny days, you may want to consider using a stabilized chlorine. Chlorine can be stabilized, or protected from the deteriorating effects of the ultraviolet rays of the sun, by adding cyanuric acid. Cyanuric acid helps to protect and "stretch" the life of chlorine. Sounds good, right? Nonetheless, stabilized chlorines are a controversial topic in the swimming pool industry.

The problem with cyanuric acid is that once it enters the pool water, it's difficult to remove. To lower the levels of cyanuric acid in pool water, you must remove old water and add fresh water. When cyanuric acid levels become greater than 100 ppm/mgl, chlorine may become bound-up and be less effective. Some people claim that when cyanuric acid levels get too high, liver and kidney damage may result. There's no agreement on exactly how much cyanuric acid is too much, however. Two of the most popular stabilized chlorines that use cyanuric acid are dichlor and trichlor. Other disadvantages of stabilized chlorines are that they can be used only in outdoor pools and that a separate test kit must be used to monitor cyanuric acid levels. Ideally, a pool's cyanuric acid levels should be between 30 to 50 ppm/mgl.

Bromine   Bromine, like chlorine, is a member of the halogen family, and has excellent disinfection and oxidation properties. Bromide is available in sticks or tablets.

The use of bromine has several advantages. Perhaps the greatest advantage is that combined bromine (bromamines) does not smell, burn, or irritate the senses the way chloramines do. Chloramines must be burned out of the water through shocking, whereas bromamines break down on their own. Bromine is also more stable than chlorine at higher water temperatures. This is why bromine is the preferred disinfectant in spas and hot tubs.

There are two major disadvantages associated with the use of bromine in pools. First, its cost relative to chlorine is a drawback; bromine typically costs twice as much. Secondly, bromine cannot be stabilized with the addition of cyanuric acid, and because it dissipates quickly in sunlight, bromine is not very suitable for outdoor pools.

■ ■ ■

OTHER DISINFECTANTS
Although chlorine is the most popular pool disinfectant and bromine is the most popular spa disinfectant, numerous other disinfectants are available that work well, too. Many of these disinfectants are becoming popular because some people would like to avoid the hazards and disadvantages of chlo-

Note how curving the pool at one end softens its large, rectangular shape. Slate coping provides a subtle yet elegant border around the perimeter of the pool. The lack of landscaping helps to keep the pool clean.

rine, or are interested in trying a different disinfectant. Although alternative disinfectants do not have the same hazards and disadvantages of chlorine, they may not disinfect or oxidize as well, either. I recommend that homeowners begin with chlorine and if they are not pleased with the results, they should then fully investigate the alternatives. Some of the more popular alternatives to chlorine and bromine include ozone, ionization, ultraviolet light, polymeric biguanide, and chlorine generation.

■ ■ ■

WATER BALANCE
While swimming pool disinfectants are used to keep pool and spa water clean, clear, and free of bacteria, pH and water balance are essential for keeping the water both com-

fortable to swimmers' eyes and skin as well as balanced to protect the pool shell, plumbing, and equipment. If pH levels are not kept within the appropriate range, the resulting unbalanced water can damage the pool shell and make the water uncomfortable to swim in. The major components of water balance are pH, total alkalinity, calcium hardness, and total dissolved solids. Chlorine and pH readings should be taken daily. Total alkalinity, calcium hardness, and total dissolved solids readings can be taken weekly or bimonthly.

pH   Many pool experts agree that pH is the most important element of swimming pool water chemistry. The lower the pH value, the more acidic the water. The higher the pH value, the more basic the water. Neutral (distilled) water has a pH of 7, but don't keep your pool or spa water neutral: keep it slightly basic, 7.2 to 7.8. The pH can be increased with a basic substance such as soda ash or lowered with acids such as muriatic acid or sodium bisulfate.

Total Alkalinity

Total alkalinity is a measure of the resistance of water to changes in pH. Total alkalinity is measured in ppms or mgls. The higher the alkalinity, the more difficult it is to change pH with either acid or soda ash. The lower the alkalinity, the more likely the pH will change; even slight changes in chemicals, swimmer loads, and weather can have a significant effect on pH or cause pH "bounce" when the alkalinity is low. If you experience difficulties either adjusting pH levels or maintaining a target pH, it's a good idea to analyze total alkalinity. Most pools should maintain total alkalinity levels between 100 and 120 ppm/mgl. Sodium bicarbonate is used to raise total alkalinity while muriatic acid or sodium bisulfate is used to lower it. When in doubt about the right alkalinity level for your particular pool, speak with your pool builder or local pool company.

Calcium Hardness

Hardness is a term often used in referring to the mineral content of the water in a swimming pool. All water supplies have varying amounts of calcium and magnesium, which make pool water hard.

Special attention must be paid to disinfection, filtration, and water balance to maintain clean, clear, and polished water.

While many people prefer it for household use, soft water can be disastrous in a swimming pool or spa. People often think they have very hard water in their homes, but chances are their water would be too "soft" for the pool. Pool water must have a high degree of hardness, otherwise the pool itself and its equipment will deteriorate. The recommended range for calcium hardness is between 200 and 500 ppm/mgl. Calcium hardness can be raised by adding calcium chloride and lowered by replacing old pool water with fresh water.

Total Dissolved Solids

As more and more chemicals are added to pool or spa water, the inactive chemical ingredients accumulate and remain dissolved there. As the water evaporates, the dissolved solids become more noticeable by clouding the

water. When filtration and chemical levels are ideal but the water has a dull, lackluster, or cloudy appearance, it's probably time to empty some or most of the pool water and replace it with fresh water that does not contain high levels of total dissolved solids.

■ ■ ■

BALANCING POOL WATER

Balanced water is neither corrosive nor scaling. Corrosive water is hungry in that it seeks "food" from the pool shell and its plumbing, and scaling water has too many ingredients, which results in residue. But if the pH, total alkalinity, and calcium hardness are kept within the recommended ranges, a pool or spa will have balanced, trouble-free water.

If, however, pool or spa water is suspected of being out of balance, the chemical values relating to water balance can be plugged in to a simple calculator or chart provided by any swimming pool service company, or you can simply do the math on the chart. A saturation index will tell you if your pool is aggressive or scale-forming. You should adjust your pool or spa to keep the water balance as close to zero as possible on this scale.

If you have what many call a "funky" or "bouncing" pool, or if your pool water is just "out of whack," it probably needs balancing. You definitely won't need a test kit to tell you this. So what is a funky, bouncing, or wacky pool? It's a pool that constantly changes. One day it's crystal clear, the next day it's cloudy. One day it's green and the next day brown. The pH levels are all over the place. If this is happening to your water, it is unbalanced. Just grab your test kit to determine which chemicals need to be adjusted to balance the pool. (See pages 124–125 for more troubleshooting tips.)

■ ■ ■

WATER TESTING

It is vital that someone test your pool and spa water faithfully, but it needn't be a chore. In fact, water testing can be fun. Youngsters can also be taught to conduct tests, and it can be quite educational. If your children are responsible for water testing, you should supervise them. (Most test procedures produce color changes that may keep your youngsters entertained.)

Test kits range from very basic to elaborate. A basic test kit should analyze the following parameters:

■ Pool disinfectant (including free, combined, and total residuals)
■ pH
■ Total alkalinity
■ Calcium hardness
■ Cyanuric acid (when applicable)

All test reagents must be kept in a cool, dark place; don't leave them out in the

Tips for Accurate Water-Testing

■ Wash your hands before and after each use of the test kit.

■ Grab a representative water sample by reaching at least 12 inches (30.5cm) down beneath the surface and away from any inlets, or artificially high readings may result.

■ Keep vials and test tubes impeccably clean to avoid false readings due to contamination.

■ Never interchange reagents of different brands and test kit models of similar brands.

■ Do not touch samples with your fingers (special caps are provided for this purpose). Do not shake samples vigorously, but swirl them gently to mix pool sample with the reagent.

■ Keep all test kits and reagents out of the reach of children and keep them in a cool, dark place.

■ Mark all your reagents with the date of purchase.

sun—surprisingly, that's where most pool owners keep them. The shelf life of many testing reagents is short (six months), and faulty readings may result if the test kit and reagents are not cared for. Be sure to purchase new reagents for each swimming season as well.

Although it may be simple and informative for you to manually perform chemical readings with your test kit, the process does take time. If this seems too tedious, you may be relieved to learn that all of the testing that is required for pool upkeep can be accomplished automatically with electronic equipment. Some of these devices not only monitor the water chemistry, but can also make the necessary chemical adjustments for you. Pool automation can greatly reduce some of the work and worry associated with maintaining a pool or spa. Ask your local swimming pool supply store for more information on pool automation for water chemistry. Chemical companies and test kit manufacturers also provide many free publications with their pool products to help you better understand pool chemistry; take advantage of their offers.

■ ■ ■

POOL EQUIPMENT

Numerous accessories are available to assist you in improving the safety, cleanliness, and enjoyment of a pool or spa—many are optional, but some are an absolute must. Pool accessories can be classified as either tools or toys, and should be thoroughly researched before building a pool. If you already own and operate a pool, some of the items, maintenance, and troubleshooting tips discussed might be helpful to keep or hand as a reference.

Pool Vacuums and Sweepers

Pool vacuums and sweepers, whether manual or automatic, are a must at most pools. The most commonly used pool tools, vacuums and sweepers are available in a variety of models and should be studied thoroughly, as not all will work efficiently in all pools. Certain pool shapes, designs, and structures can stop the vacuum in its tracks or even turn it on its back. When an automatic pool vacuum "turtles up," it can lie motionless for hours without accomplishing any cleaning. If you do not want to bother with pool vacuuming, sweeping, or purchasing additional equipment, hire a local swimming pool service company to provide this mandatory maintenance. Whether you perform this important chore or someone else does, if the interior shell is not kept clean and free of debris during the swimming season, the pool will look and feel dirty, algae and bacteria growth will increase, and as a result, more chemicals will need to be used to oxidize organics in the pool. Regardless of the type of vacuum you use, a vacuum head with brushes attached is a good idea because brushing and vacuuming can take place simultaneously.

Manual vacuums are pushed by hand with long extension poles. They are usually powered by suction generated by the circulation system. The manual vacuum incorporates a vacuum head, a flexible vacuum hose, and a long extension pole to push the head across the pool bottom. One end of the flexible hose connects to the head, while the other end fits into the surface skimmer. In this fashion, the circulation system provides strong suction for the vacuum. Other manual vacuums are powered by electricity or gas, but these older models are not as popular as those that are plugged in to the surface skimmer.

When linked to your pool circulation system, vacuums can be powered either by the suction side or the pressure side of the pool pump. Suction-side cleaners have the advantage of not using additional power—electricity, special plumbing, or booster pumps are unnecessary as these vacuums receive enough suction from the existing filtration system. Pool debris can be sent to the skimmer, to the filter, or directly to waste, depending upon the circumstances.

Nonetheless, automatic vacuums are rapidly replacing manual suction-side vacuums. Unlike the manual model that must be pushed by hand with a long extension pole, the automatic vacuum uses recirculating pool water to propel it hydraulically. Many swimming pool service companies, however, tend to use manual vacuums. This is because automatic cleaners wander along the bottom of the pool, requiring more time (but none of your time) to complete the job than do manual vacuums.

Pressure-side pool vacuums are similar to their suction-side counterparts, except that they create suction by using a sucking action provided by the pressure side of the circulation system. In this case, pool water is pushed down into the vacuum head and up into a collection bag. This action creates suction that pulls water and debris up from the pool bottom and into the vacuum bag. When vacuuming is complete, the vacuum bag must be emptied and cleaned, but at least this dirt does not end up in the filter. Some pressure-side vacuums require a booster pump to provide sufficient water power for good vacuuming suction. They can be pushed by hand, but most homeowners prefer to use self-propelled vacuums.

Jet cleaners, or jet vacuums, use a garden hose, with or without a booster pump, to create a venturi suction and draw debris up into a vacuum bag. A jet cleaner does not use the pool circulation for suction nor does it deposit dirt into the filter. Jet cleaners are simple, inexpensive manual vacuum cleaners that are used by many service companies and homeowners.

Some vacuums are powered by electricity and contain a motor, gear box, and drive belts. These electric vacuums resemble underwater robots and do an excellent job of roaming the bottom, picking up dirt and other debris. Like the other self-propelled vacuums, pool robots catch dirt by traveling randomly along the bottom. They are powered by electricity, so no one should be in the pool when they are in use. A malfunction could cause serious electric shock.

Pool sweepers are used to clean pool bottoms and walls, too. Pool sweepers are

This pool complements the formal garden by providing a blue backdrop for pink flowers. Limited deck space and extensive foliage, however, indicates that this pool is more form than function.

Daily Chores The pool surface should be cleaned with a leaf skimmer to remove any airborne debris on a daily basis. Otherwise, debris will become saturated with water, sink to the bottom, and thus become difficult to remove.

Surface debris also finds its way into the surface skimmer outlets. Surface skimmer baskets must be cleaned daily as well, or the pool's circulation and filtration systems will become impaired.

All chemical levels in the pool should be tested on a daily basis, most particularly chlorine and pH. If the pool is going to be filled with many swimmers, plan on testing the water several times a day.

The pool should also be brushed for a few minutes every day. This will reduce weekly vacuuming time and prevent algae from growing on the pool shell. Always brush toward the main drain, and try to brush in the early hours of the morning after all the debris has settled to the bottom. The best-kept pool shells are usually brushed regularly.

attractive water hoses that are attached to the return inlets in the pool or added to an automatic vacuum roaming the bottom. Some sweepers require a booster pump (an extra pump that is used when household pressure is low) to produce sufficient water pressure to work well, but simply use the returning water in the circulation system. Sweepers are agitating hoses that whip across the bottom and sides of the pool, constantly spraying water to push dirt toward the main drain, where the dirt is removed from the pool by the ever-present suction. Floating sweepers can also be installed to keep the surface clean.

Automatic pool vacuums and sweepers work well together. Don't swim during vacuuming; it is impractical and unsafe. Swimming action stirs up the dirt, making it more difficult to catch, and swimmers can become entangled in the hoses.

■ ■ ■

POOL MAINTENANCE

Pool maintenance chores must be done regularly to avoid problems such as poor water clarity, algae growth, and chlorine production and to protect your investment. Some

Weekly Chores The pool should be vacuumed once a week if you want to keep the pool bottom clean. You may have to do this more often if you have a lot of plants

Colored tile beautifies this pool setting. The raised tiles surrounding the pool elevate the pool and enhance its reflective qualities.

surrounding your pool. Vacuuming should also be done immediately following inclement weather.

There's nothing worse than a "bathtub ring" on the sides of a beautiful swimming pool. At least once a week, this scum line should be wiped off with an approved cleaner, one that is compatible with your vinyl, fiberglass, or tile finish. Many household cleaners are suitable, but check with your pool supply store first.

Cleaning or backwashing the filter should be done weekly, or as necessary if the pool is busy, to ensure good water clarity and protect the pool equipment.

Shocking, or superchlorination, should also be done weekly to prevent algae growth and chloramine production. Shocking regularly will also burn up a lot of organic debris, thereby assisting your filter in keeping the water clean. Shocking is good preventive maintenance for pool water and should not be overlooked.

The pool deck should be hosed down and cleaned once a week, too. You might want to use an algicide or higher chlorine levels if you have algae beginning to take hold. Other accessories, such as diving boards and slides, should also be cleaned on a weekly basis.

■ ■ ■

SOLVING COMMON POOL PROBLEMS

A properly planned and maintained pool is virtually trouble-free—or should be. But problems do occur. Weather, source water, equipment malfunction, and human error are the usual causes for pool problems. To follow are common problems—and what to do about them.

Cloudy, Milky Water

Cloudy, milky water is a frequent problem at some pools, and its cause is often the neglect of the pool's circulation or disinfection system.

Cloudy, milky water can have many causes. Fortunately, there is a step-by-step plan for narrowing down the sources of the problem. The first step to correct the situation is to check the chemical disinfectant levels. A low quantity of disinfectant in the pool will quickly turn a pool cloudy. If you find there is enough chlorine in the water, check the pump. If the pump is not running, the water is not being filtered; this could simply be a tripped circuit breaker or a loose connection. If you can't get the pump started, though, call your pool service company or an electrician. In addition, a clogged hair and lint strainer will also stop circulation and filtration. Air bubbles may also be getting into these systems through a loose lid on the hair and lint strainer, causing aeration of the pool water. The pool filter may also need cleaning. If you have a DE filter, make sure the DE is not returning to the pool; if it is, it will turn the water milky white. Finally, check the water balance. If any one of the chemical parameters is out of line, cloudiness may result.

Malodorous, Irritating Water

If your pool water smells like chlorine, burns the eyes, or irritates the skin, there are probably high combined chlorine levels in the pool. Take free, total, and combined chlorine readings, then shock your pool with an amount of chlorine that is ten times greater than the combined reading. Eye irritation may also be caused by a low pH or unbalanced water, so when necessary, the pH should be raised and the water balanced.

Green Water

Green water is usually caused by algae. Shock the pool, and if you anticipate more problems, add an algicide. Brushing the pool helps prevent algae growth, although pools in warm climates have significant algae growth and may require a regular prevention plan.

Red or Brown Water

Red or brown water is usually caused by high iron content in the source water. To fix the situation, you'll need to obtain a sequestering agent or a clarifier to control the iron levels. In older pools and homes, red or brown water may be caused by rusty pipes, so this may be a recurring problem, particularly when you're filling the pool at the beginning of each swimming season.

Blue-Green Water

If it's not caused by algae, blue-green water is often due to a high copper content in the water makeup or highly aggressive water corroding copper pipes and heater elements. Balance the water and use a sequestering or chelating agent, available from your local swimming pool dealer.

Blue or Black Water

Water that is blue or black usually indicates that there is manganese in your swimming pool water. Corrosive water is more likely to bring out this substance. This situation can be remedied in the same fashion as just described for water that has a too-high iron or copper content.

Pump Problems

If the pool pump is noisy or running hot, turn off the motor immediately to prevent further damage. The bearings may be going bad. Call a pool service technician.

Sand in the Pool

If you find sand in the pool, particularly under the inlets, it's probably coming from the filter. An oversized pool pump or a cracked lateral (underdrain) in your filter could be causing this, or there may be too much sand in the filter. Call your swimming pool service contractor.

Excessive Water Loss

If the pool seems to be losing a lot of water, and you don't think this is due to evaporation, your pool may have a leak. If you have a vinyl-lined pool, check your entire liner carefully. If you find a hole or cut, you can repair it yourself. The most likely place for a leak in all types of pools is the main drain, but this is a problem that can only be fixed by a professional. Many sophisticated leak-detection systems are available from your pool service company.

Excessive Foaming

Foaming is more likely to occur in spas and hot tubs than in swimming pools. Soft water (low calcium hardness), algicides, and high total dissolved solids caused by lotions, creams, shampoos, and the like can all cause excessive foaming. It's definitely a good idea to balance your water before purchasing a defoamer. Pranksters have also been known to add detergents to spas, hot tubs, and swimming pools.

■ ■ ■

Keeping the pool water balanced and maintaining appropriate disinfecting levels will prevent most pool problems. However, if something out of the ordinary does occur and this problem-solving information does not offer you a solution, it's time to call in a swimming pool service company. If you find that balancing the water is too much trouble, contract with a pool professional to do it for you.

Chapter Six

Barriers

Swimming pool barriers are a relatively new concept in the swimming pool industry. For our purposes, an effective barrier is a fence, safety cover, wall, alarm, sensor, or combination of structures that completely surrounds or covers the pool and/or spa and prevents unauthorized entry. Barriers are not intended solely for protection, however. Barriers also help to ensure privacy; protection from intruders; safety, by preventing young children from entering the pool; and conservation, by saving water, heat, and chemicals. Many municipalities have pool barrier requirements.

In many areas, drowning in residential swimming pools is the leading cause of accidental death around the home for children under five. Effective barriers are one of the best ways to protect children, as it is almost impossible for parents to keep youngsters in sight 100 percent of the time. Barriers are not intended, however, to take the place of vigilant supervision. I hope that the ideas for barriers that are presented here will save lives, money, and valuable resources.

■ ■ ■

WALLS AND FENCES

Walls and fences were discussed from a landscaping perspective in chapter one; they will be discussed now from a security standpoint. Fences and walls along the perimeter of the property serve several functions. They add privacy, protect against trespassers, and prevent young children from wandering into the pool. An ideal height for barriers on the perimeter of the yard is 6 to 8 feet (1.8 to 2.4m). Fences that are 6 to 8 feet high are difficult to climb and almost impossible to peer over.

Check your local codes before installing any perimeter barrier. Some municipalities may require 8-foot barriers on the perimeter of the property, and other areas may have height restrictions. Some regions may require a perimeter barrier on all four sides of the pool, not permitting the house to serve as one side of the barrier. This is because children have been known to crawl out of windows and doors to get to the pool. In areas where the house is permitted to serve as one side of the barrier, locks and alarms should be installed on all windows and doors facing the pool to prevent children from entering the swimming area unnoticed. All hinged doors, sliding doors, and windows of the house should have self-latching devices that are at least 56 inches (1.4m) above the floor to prevent small children from opening them.

When safety and security are the primary functions of the perimeter barrier, the fence or wall must be difficult to climb and be free of handholds and footholds. Tables, chairs, benches, trees, rocks, or anything else that can be used to help scale the fence should be removed from the area as well. If the barrier is composed of vertical slats, the slats must not be more than 4 inches (10.2cm) apart, or a child may be able to squeeze through the openings. When chain-

White, open fencing may bring color out of the garden and define the edge of the pool deck, but it does not provide security nor does it prevent debris from entering the pool.

link fencing is used, the diamond-shaped openings should be less than 1 inch (2.5cm) across. As a rule of thumb, no fence should permit a 4-inch cube to pass anywhere through the structure. All gates and doors must have a self-closing and self-latching mechanism that is out of the reach of children. Where the risk of unauthorized entry is high, doors and gates can be installed with audio and visual alarms.

Many water-safety experts and home-owners prefer double barriers: one wall on the perimeter of the lot, and one near the pool. Fencing near the pool should be approximately 4 feet (1.2m) high and must be see-through, so that views of the pool are not obstructed and supervision is not compromised in any manner. Remember,

it is essential that the entire barrier be childproof.

Protective barriers give many above-ground pools an advantage. Because one must climb over the side wall of an above-ground pool to gain access to the water, many above-ground pools come with retractable ladders that can be pulled up over the side of the pool and locked into place when not in use. The ladder is then incorporated into a perimeter fence that lies on top of the pool wall and decking. The above-ground pool fence must never be a platform to walk, stand, or sit on. All entries into the water from the barrier must be banned, particularly headfirst entries.

Fencing is another big ticket item. If you want complete privacy and security, you

could spend a small fortune on fencing. And if small children will be in the vicinity of or using the pool, fencing is not an area to skimp on. Before purchasing any fence, make certain that it meets all requirements of your local swimming pool code, including height (usually 4 feet [1.2m]), spacing of pickets (usually 4 inches [10.2cm]), and type of gates (self-closing and self-latching).

Fencing costs can range from as little as $4 per linear foot ($13 per m) for inexpensive chain-link fence to as much as $60 per foot ($197 per m) for decorative iron or aluminum. As the number of gates installed increases, so will the price. Likewise, slopes in the yard will also add to the cost of the fence. An average-size swimming pool will typically require about 150 feet (45.7m) of fence that is 4 feet (1.2m) tall just outside the pool deck. If your municipality allows the house to serve as one side of the fence, you could save about 25 percent in the cost of the fence, but in the end you could end up paying more, as alarms on doors and windows facing the pool may then be necessary. If you are also considering perimeter fencing around the yard for privacy and security, a taller, more expensive fence will be required; an average-size yard may need 200 to 300 feet (61 to 91.4m) of fence.

For safety reasons, I always recommend some type of fence. When selecting a fence, remember to consider what will work in terms of security (fencing close to the pool should not obstruct the view of the water) and privacy, what will enhance your poolscape aesthetically, and what you can afford—but be careful; this is one purchase you cannot put off until later. Your fence should be in place before you fill your pool with water.

If there are no financial constraints concerning fencing material, I would recommend iron or PVC because of their great looks and durability. If you have an open landscaping design and are convinced that security and privacy are not large concerns, you can save a significant amount of money if you don't install a fence. But if you elect not to have a fence, don't be surprised if you have privacy and safety problems, such as trespassers and a range of assorted critters.

COVERS

Pool and spa covers are intended to prevent children and unwanted persons from entering the water, and to prevent the water from evaporating. Most covers can be set in place either manually or automatically and are usually made of nylon or vinyl. Automatic pool covers save a lot of work. There are so many types of covers it is easy to become confused when deciding what to purchase. The following should help.

Hard-top covers are covers that rest on the lip of the pool or spa deck and do not float on the surface of the water. Hard-top

Automatic pool covers provide a great margin of safety for pool owners and should be considered a standard piece of equipment in most pool packages.

covers block the pool from unauthorized entry, keep unsightly airborne debris out of the water, and provide thermal protection by helping the water to retain heat. Like other covers, hard-top covers reduce water evaporation and chemical loss.

Winter covers are relatively inexpensive and are secured around the perimeter of a pool or spa when it is closed for the season. Winter covers provide a barrier for debris only, and most will not support the weight of people or pets. If covering the pool is a safety concern, you may want to purchase a security cover rather than a winter cover, which would be safer yet still protect the pool. These covers must be secured well along their perimeter with either water bags or hooks and straps. A disadvantage of solid

winter covers is that they can collect a lot of surface water, which may endanger children and pets as well as make them extremely difficult to remove.

Solar covers are one of the most popular pool accessories used to increase water temperature. They are placed on the surface when the pool is not in use during the day so that the heat will be retained during the evening. These covers may also help reduce water and chemical loss through evaporation by placing a barrier between the water and the air. To a lesser extent, solar covers also keep debris out of the pool. Solar covers will not support the weight of people or pets and must be completely removed before anyone swims in the pool. This is a fact that cannot be overstated.

Thermal covers are similar to solar covers, except that they prevent evaporation and heat loss instead of heating the water. The cost of both solar and thermal covers can often be recovered during the first swimming season because of the savings they provide.

Safety covers are intended to reduce the risk of drowning for children under five by preventing them from entering the pool. Safety covers must be properly anchored to the perimeter of the pool. They do not allow water to collect on the surface because they are made of a flow-through mesh material. Safety covers should support a minimum of 30 pounds per square foot (146.5kg per sq m). A true safety cover must pass standards set forth by testing laboratories and will be marked as such. Safety covers can also be used when winterizing your pool.

■ ■ ■

ALARMS AND SENSORS

Alarms and electronic sensors are considered safety barriers, as they help prevent children and others from entering pools, hot tubs, and spas. Alarms can be placed inside the house, pool, or both. If you have young children, you should consider using these warning devices.

In-pool alarms emit a loud signal whenever the water is disturbed. This is extremely helpful at times when the pool is

With a pool this close to the house, it is critical that alarms or sensors be installed to prevent accidents, particularly if children will be using the pool.

closed; the alarm can simply be turned off when it is open. One type of in-pool alarm floats in the pool and reacts to surface tension or activity. This wave-motion alarm alerts you when something or someone falls in (or enters) the water, disturbing the still water surface. Two-part electronic detection sensors are also available: an underwater component remains in the pool, and a wristband or necklace is worn by a person. If that person falls into the pool, the underwater sensor sets off an alarm. Photoelectric eyes, similar to those used for security in buildings, can also work well at swimming pools by establishing invisible light beams all around the pool. When the beam is interrupted, a loud alarm goes off. In a similar fashion, infrared sensors can be used to detect body heat and will sound an alarm accordingly.

You can purchase a complete surveillance system for the pool, including television cameras and microphones that are transmitted into the house. You may also want to consider installing an alarm inside the house to alert you when a child suddenly wanders outside. Consult your pool supplier or home improvement center to see what is available in your area. Although there are many types of alarms for the home, perhaps the most practical are those similar to antitheft alarms for cars. All doors and windows should be wired so that whenever they are opened, a loud buzzer or siren will sound. An alarm switch or keypad to turn off the system should be conveniently located but placed high enough on a wall so that it is out of the reach of children. All alarms and sensors should be turned on and checked daily. A faulty alarm or one that is not turned on will not help you in preventing accidents.

It is very important to develop a system of barriers to protect your investment as well as your family. But remember, no barrier or alarm is foolproof. Fences, barriers, covers, and alarms can often give the pool owner a false sense of security. Constant, vigilant supervision is the best way to prevent pool accidents. This is another area of your pool project that requires thorough consideration.

Chapter Seven

Safety

Pools are built to enhance the quality of life and to improve fitness, but whenever a body of water exists in or around a residence, risks increase. The purpose of this chapter is to provide you with information that can help to ensure pool safety. Although numerous safety signs, practices, and apparatuses are presented here, there is no substitute for close supervision. Vigilant supervision and the use of safety practices, barriers, and equipment form the best combination for swimming pool safety.

■ ■ ■

POOL RULES

Rules for the swimming pool must be established before your pool or spa is filled with water. These rules should be dictated by the age and skill level of the people using the pool. Although fun is important, swimming pool behavior must never become boisterous. Many a pool accident has been precipitated by playful roughhousing. Commonsense rules must be posted and enforced. Some of the more common pool rules include:

■ **Never Swim Alone.** This rule applies to both children and adults. The buddy system must be strongly encouraged, and even nonswimmers can be rescuers if they use good judgment and if lifesaving equipment is available at poolside.
■ **No Glass or Breakables Permitted in the Pool Area.** Broken glass in or around a pool can lead to serious wounds.

■ **No Swimming with Open Cuts, Sores, or Infections.** There is the distinct possibility that bacteria and other chemicals found in the pool water may make the open wounds worse, and other swimmers can become infected as well.

■ **No Swimming When the Bottom at the Deep End Cannot Be Seen Clearly.** In this case, if a swimmer is in trouble under the surface, he or she will go unnoticed.

■ **Children Under Twelve Must Be Closely Supervised by an Adult.** Unsupervised youngsters around a pool are less capable of protecting and rescuing themselves.

■ **No More Than ____ People in the Pool at One Time.** Posting the swimmer capacity is important because overcrowded pools can easily lead to accidents due to collisions and inadequate supervision.

■ **No Running.** Running often leads to slipping and falling, which can result in injury.

■ **No Diving.** Diving from the deck should be allowed only when there is a minimum of 6 feet (1.8m) of water.

■ **No Sliding Headfirst.** Very serious head, neck, and back injuries can result if sliding headfirst is permitted.

■ **No Extended Breath-Holding Underwater.** Underwater swims combined with breath-holding for long periods of time must be discouraged. Underwater swimming and breath-holding is a popular pool game, but unfortunately, the activity can cause unconsciousness underwater due to a carbon dioxide deficiency in the bloodstream. This is the result of hyperventilation that occurs during these very dangerous underwater games.

■ ■ ■

SAFEGUARDING CHILDREN

Toddlers between the ages of one and three are the ones most likely to drown in residential pools. Also, many near-drowning victims are sent to hospital emergency rooms each year. Therefore, extra efforts must be taken to protect children around the pool.

Young children enter swimming pools quickly and quietly. Children in trouble in the water cannot cry out for help because all of their energy is spent attempting to breathe. For this reason, safeguarding children around a swimming pool requires a complete safety system—a combination of safety equipment and techniques. No single safety practice or piece of equipment is foolproof. If children will be using your pool, develop a series of safety practices so that if one technique fails, another technique or apparatus can readily be put into effect.

Flotation devices can develop confidence in young children in the water but must never become a substitute for close parental supervision.

Teaching Young Children to Swim

Having a pool in the yard provides benefits for everyone, particularly young children. Infants and toddlers become more comfortable in water when the surroundings are familiar and nonthreatening.

When working with young children, it must be understood that breath control, relaxation, fun, praise, and encouragement are more important than perfecting stroke mechanics. Introducing youngsters to the water early and often is vital to swimming success. The Red Cross, YMCA, and other agencies provide a wealth of information on teaching children to swim and on water safety in general. Consult the resources in the back of this book for further information.

Supervision It's a fact: a child can drown in less than one minute.

The most effective way for parents to protect their children from drowning in their own backyard is to practice vigilant supervision. Engaging in other activities like reading, barbecuing, or gardening while children are in the pool is not considered adequate supervision. Children often drown while the parent leaves the pool area to answer the phone. In fact, parents of most young drowning victims claim they left their child unsupervised in or by the pool for less than five minutes.

Don't ever let this happen to you. Don't ever leave children alone around a pool for any length of time, and when you're at the pool, don't get distracted or let your friends get distracted from watching your or their children.

Flotation devices are not a substitute for supervision, either. Inflatable swimming aids can deflate or even slip off the child.

Toys and other swimming accessories must not be left in or around the pool. When the pool is not in use, all toys, balls, and floats should be removed, for toys and the like can lure unsupervised children into the water. Additionally, a pool deck cluttered with furniture and toys can obstruct the view of the water, thus impairing supervision and delaying rescue efforts.

Remember, these safety precautions could prevent a tragedy. Practice them faithfully, and your pool will be a safer place.

ADULT CONCERNS

Preventing adults from entering shallow water headfirst is a major concern. Entering shallow water headfirst produces more cases of permanent paralysis than all other sport activities combined. It must be emphasized, however, that these injuries rarely occur from diving boards but rather from docks, decks, and other platforms. Adults need at least 6 feet (1.8m) of water in order to make a safe headfirst entry from the deck into a pool, although many safety groups are now calling for 9-foot (2.7m) diving depths. If you have a diving board, it would be wise to limit its use to children under twelve.

Excessive drinking around the pool can also lead to diving and other water accidents. Drowning is also a possibility for adults, although the risk is less than it is for children. And as already mentioned, the buddy system helps in preventing accidents for adults and children alike.

SAFETY AND RESCUE EQUIPMENT

The Telephone

The telephone is perhaps the most important piece of safety equipment. A telephone should always be at poolside, and it should remain in a desig-

Inflatable rings not only are used as toys but can double as life-saving equipment when the need arises. When the pool is not in use, the rings should be removed so they don't lure small children into the pool.

nated area that is clearly marked. Emergency numbers must also be listed by the phone. It is best to install a separate phone that is enclosed in some way, or to install a weatherproof phone. If this is not practical, a portable or plug-in phone may be used at the pool, but it must remain in a designated area. Nothing is worse than hunting for the phone during a crisis—it's a loss of valuable seconds. 911 or other rescue numbers should be boldly displayed on or near your phone as well. A conspicuous "PHONE" sign should be posted so that neighbors or friends can find it easily during an emergency, and complete emergency procedures should be listed there as well.

Another important function of the poolside telephone is that a supervisor does not need to be inside to answer the phone and leave children unsupervised momentarily. You should never leave the pool area to answer the phone when children are anywhere near the water.

Flotation Devices/Lifelines

Flotation devices are a good idea for children and novice adult swimmers, but should never take the place of supervision. Flotation aids used for safety should be the type that are zipped or tied onto the swimmer so as to not slip off. Solid flotation devices that cannot be deflated are better than those that are filled with air. Flotation devices that encompass the entire upper torso are also more effective than those that fit only the back or upper arms.

Lifelines are ropes with buoys attached to them. A lifeline floats on the surface of the pool and is most often placed between the shallow and deep portions of the pool to prevent children and adult nonswimmers from slipping into water that is over their heads. The lifeline should be placed 2 to 3 feet (0.6–0.9m) in front of the slope leading to deep water.

Rescue Equipment

Whether a child or an adult is in distress, entering the water is recommended only as a last resort, as a double drowning may result because of the drowning person's frantic attempts to stay above water. Instead, every effort should be made to rescue the person by using equipment.

Many excellent rescue devices are available. They can be purchased, and many of them can be made at home. Some of the more popular and easy-to-use rescue devices include:

- **Long, Light Reaching Pole.** This pole should be 10 to 12 feet (3 to 3.7m) long. A pole with a rounded end is called a "shepherd's" crook.
- **Ring Buoy.** The ring buoy must be sufficiently buoyant to maintain two adults on the surface. Ring buoys often come with a throwing line attached to them, although ring buoys without throwing lines can also be used. In this case, the ring buoy is pushed or swum out to the victim.
- **Throwing Line.** This line must reach across the width of the pool and should be 30 to 40 feet long (9.1 to 12.2m). Many homeowners use a rope attached to a gallon (3.8l) plastic jug that contains a couple of inches (about 5cm) of water. The weight of the water aids in throwing the jug to the victim.
- **Standard First-Aid Kit.** This kit should include items used to stop bleeding, like compresses. Bee-sting medication and Band-Aids are always helpful to have on hand, as are chemical ice packs.

CPR   During a water crisis, every second can make the difference between life and death. CPR (cardiopulmonary resuscitation) should be learned and reviewed by all residential pool owners so that if necessary, it can be performed while waiting for the rescue squad. Classes in this lifesaving technique are available through local Red Cross chapters and heart associations.

■ ■ ■

OTHER SAFETY MEASURES

Barriers   The swimming pool industry has made great strides in the development of protective barriers for swimming pools (see chapter six). When using a pool cover, you must remove it completely before anyone enters the water. Winds can blow a partially removed pool cover onto a swimmer, causing entrapment.

Electrical Safety   All electrical outlets located near the pool should be covered and protected by ground-fault circuit interrupters (GFI) to prevent electrical shock. A licensed electrician should perform all electrical work and repairs around the pool and in the filter room. All swimming pool wiring should conform to building and electrical codes. All electrical appliances, including radios and televisions, should be

kept dry and well away from the water. A minimum distance of 5 feet (1.5m) is best. If appliances must be used near the pool, battery-operated alternatives are recommended. When you make minor electrical repairs around the pool, be sure to turn the pool power off first.

Electrical repairs in a wet environment can be risky. For this reason, hire a licensed electrician. Repairing underwater lights requires an expert. Never attempt to do this yourself.

Chemical Safety   First and foremost, swimming pool chemicals must be kept out of the reach of children. In addition, pool chemicals must be stored separately; storing pool chemicals in a garage, basement, or all-purpose shed is not a good idea. This is because fertilizers, petroleum products, soft drinks, and many other household supplies can combine with many pool chemicals, causing fires or explosions.

When transporting chemicals from store to home, use a separate cardboard or plastic box to protect the car and passengers from chemical spills. Pool chemicals should never be left unattended in a car. Upon arriving home, quickly and carefully move the chemicals to their proper storage area. (See chapter five for helpful safety tips on chemical storage.)

Make sure you read and understand the directions before using any pool chemicals.

Both natural and manufactured shade make these poolside surroundings more pleasant. The canopy, however, does not serve as protection from unsafe conditions such as storms, lightning, and high winds.

tant pool topics, including safety. They may also publish quality videos. It's worth your while to investigate safety-oriented books, magazines, and the like. Although a pool may be soundly built, beautifully landscaped, and accessorized to the hilt, it is nothing if safety is not the first priority.

■ ■ ■

The Swimming Pool was written to help novice and experienced pool owners to plan, operate, and, of course, enjoy their swimming pools. The book is meant to be a source of information and inspiration, and I hope you will look to it for both answers and ideas. Bear in mind, though, despite the abundance of material covered here, nothing can replace consulting builders and other pool owners to get a clear picture of what is vital to constructing and maintaining a successful pool project. Perhaps the greatest help to planning and operating a swimming pool is finding a local pool service company that is both knowledgeable and dependable. And above all, remember that a successful pool project takes time: never rush into building a pool. Do all your homework first.

Today, the pool options are many. In fact, there is a pool for almost any yard and budget. With careful research, thoughful planning, and a little ingenuity, you can enjoy a clean, clear, safe, and beautiful pool of your very own.

Chemicals must never be mixed together, and the same scoop should not be used for different chemicals. Pool chemicals should not be added to the pool when swimmers are in the water. You should also wear eye, hand, and face protection when working with chemicals, and when dilution is required, add chemicals to water rather than adding water to chemicals.

Pool Closure   Whenever an unsafe condition or hazard exists in or around your pool, close the pool immediately. When there are storms, high winds, and lightning, swimmers are facing considerable risks, so they should leave the pool area. When there is lightning, not only should you close the pool, but you should make sure everyone at the pool moves into the house and consults local weather forecasters for storm information. Other unsafe conditions that require immediate closure of the pool include broken glass, fallen electrical wires, cloudy pool water, and a lack of disinfectant or filtration.

The Red Cross and your local trade organizations should have excellent publications for pool owners on a variety of impor-

PLANTS FOR THE POOL

Although a swimming pool can be built in just about any climate, plants, unfortunately, are not nearly as versatile. Before selecting plants for your poolscape, be sure to consult your local nursery or gardening center for recommendations for your region. A visit to a few neighboring pools might also be a good way to get ideas as well as to determine what plants may work for your pool.

The plants listed below are suggested for poolscape because they will not cause injury, do not cause objectionable odors, and are not prone to littering your landscape with berries, pods, or leaves. These plants also have shallow, fibrous root systems that will not clog piping or disrupt decks.

Plants for General Use

PERENNIALS

Achillea filipendulina	Fern-leaf yarrow
Alyssum montanum	Madwort
Astilbe spp.	Spiraea
Coreopsis spp.	Tickseed
Delphinium spp.	Delphinium
Dianthus Caryophyllus	Carnation
Gazania spp.	Gazania
Gypsophilia paniculata	Baby's-breath
Hemerocallis spp.	Daylily
Heuchera sanguinea	Coralbell
Hosta spp.	Plantain lily
Iberis sempervirens	Edging candytuft
Iris spp.	Iris
Lavandula angustifolia	English lavender
Liriope spicata	Creeping lilyturf
Phlox subulata	Moss phlox
Rudbeckia hirta	Black-eyed Susan
Santolina Chamaecyparissus	Lavender cotton
Sedum spp.	Sedum

COVERS

Ground Covers

Cornus canadensis	Bunchberry
Euonymus radicans	Winter creeper
Fern spp.	Ferns
Hedera Helix	English ivy
Hemerocallis spp.	Daylily
Hosta spp.	Plantain lily
Phalaris arundinacea var. *picta*	Ribbon grass
Viola spp.	Violet

Evergreen Ground Covers

Asarum europaeum	European ginger
Euonymus Fortunei 'Colorata'	Purple winter creeper
Gaultheria procumbens	Wintergreen
Iberis sempervirens	Candytuft
Juniperus chinensis var. *sargentii*	Japanese garden juniper or Sargent juniper
Juniperus horizontalis	Creeping juniper
Leucothoe Fontanesiana	Drooping juniper
Pachysandra terminalis	Japanese spurge
Sedum spurium	Goldmoss stonecrop
Vinca minor	Periwinkle or myrtle

Herbaceous Perennial Ground Covers

Achillea Millefolium 'Rosea'	Pink yarrow
Arabis procurrens	Rock cress
Convallaria majalis	Lily-of-the-valley
Dianthus spp.	Dianthus

Ornamental Grasses

Armeria maritima	Sea pink
Arundo Donax	Giant reed
Festuca ovina var. *glauca*	Blue fescue
Miscanthus sinensis	Eulalia grass
Pennisetum setaceum	Fountain grass

VINES

Deciduous Vines

Akebia quinata	Five-leaf akebia
Campsis radicans	Trumpet creeper
Clematis dioscoreifolia var. *robusta*	Sweet autumn clematis
Clematis montana	Pink clematis
Parthenocissus quinquefolia	Virginia creeper
Parthenocissus tricuspidata	Boston ivy
Wisteria floribunda	Japanese wisteria

Evergreen Vines

Euonymus fortunei vars.	Winter creeper
Hedera Helix	English ivy

DECIDUOUS ORNAMENTAL SHRUBS

Small Shrubs (up to 5 feet [1.5m] at mature height, approximately)

Abeliophyllum distichum	Korean white forsythia
Comptonia peregrina	Sweet fern
Cornus sericea 'Flaviramea'	Golden-twig dogwood
Cornus sericea 'Kelseyi'	Dwarf red-osier dogwood
Cotoneaster apiculatus	Cranberry cotoneaster
Euonymus alata 'Compacta'	Dwarf winged spindle tree
Forsythia viridissima 'Bronxensis'	Bronx forsythia
Fothergilla Gardenii	Witch alder
Kerria japonica 'Pleniflora'	Japanese rose
Potentilla fruticosa	Shrubby cinqufoil
Spiraea japonica 'Alpina'	Japanese spiraea
Spiraea nipponica	Tosa spiraea
Stephananadra incisa	Lace shrub
Viburnum Opulus 'Nanum'	Dwarf European cranberry bush

Medium Shrubs (5 to 10 feet [1.5 to 3m] at mature height, approximately)

Aronia arbutifolia	Red chokeberry
Clethra alinifolia	Summer-sweet
Cornus alba 'Sibirica'	Siberian dogwood
Forsythia intermedia 'Spectabilis'	Golden-bells forsythia
Forsythia suspensa var. *Sieboldi*	Weeping forsythia
Fothergilla major	Large witch alder
Hamamelis vernalis	Vernal witch alder

Ilex verticillata	Winterberry
Myrica pensylvanica	Bayberry
Rhododendron calendulaceum	Flame azalea
Rhododendron 'Exbury Hybrid'	Exbury hybrid azalea
Rhododendron × gandavense	Ghent hybrid azalea
Rhododendron 'Jane Abbott Hybrid'	Jane Abbott hybrid azalea
Rhododendron prinophyllum	Rose-shell or early azalea
Rhododendron Schlippenbachii	Royal azalea
Rhododendron Vaseyi	Pink-shell azalea
Rhododendron viscosum	Swamp azalea
Spiraea prunifolia	Bridal wreath
Viburnum × Burkwoodii	Burkwood viburnum
Viburnum Carlesii	Korean spice viburnum
Viburnum dilatatum	Linden viburnum
Viburnum Opulus 'Roseum'	Snowball bush
Viburnum plicatum formatomentosum	Double-file viburnum

Large Shrubs (over 10 feet [3m] at mature height, approximately)

Cornus mas	Cornelian cherry dogwood
Cornus racemosa	Panicled dogwood
Corylopsis glabrescens	Winter hazel
Euonymus alata	Winged spindle tree
Hamamelis mollis	Chinese witch hazel
Hamamelis virginiana	Common witch hazel
Viburnum dentatum	Arrowwood

EVERGREENS

Evergreen Trees

Juniperus chinensis var. *procumbus 'Nana'*	Japanese garden juniper
Pinus Strobus	White pine
Taxus cuspidata 'Nana'	Dwarf Japanese yew
Tsuga canadensis	Canadian hemlock

Broad-Leaved Evergreens

Kalmia latifolia vars.	Mountain laurel
Leucothoe axillaris	Coast leucothoe
Leucothoe Fontanesiana	Drooping leucothoe
Pieris floribunda	Fetterbush
Pieris japonica 'Compacta'	Dwarf Japanese andromeda
Rhododendron 'Boule de Neige'	Boule de Neige rhododendron

Rhododendron carolinianum	Carolina rhododendron
Rhododendron catawbiense vars.	Catawba rhododendron
Rhododendron 'Chionoides'	Chionoides rhododendron
Rhododendron 'Delaware Valley white'	Delaware Valley white azalea
Rhododendron Fortunei 'Scintillation'	Scintillation rhododendron
Rhododendron Kaempferi 'Herbert'	Herbert azalea
Rhododendron × laetevirens	Wilson rhododendron
Rhododendron maximum	Great laurel rhododendron
Rhododendron 'Nova Zembla'	Nova Zembla rhododendron
Rhododendron obtusum 'Hinocrimson'	Hinocrimson azalea
Rhododendron obtusum 'Hinodegiri'	Hinodegiri azalea
Rhododendron 'P.J.M. Hybrids'	P.J.M. hybrid rhododendron
Rhododendron 'Purple Gem'	Purple gem rhododendron

Evergreen Shrubs

Ilex crenata 'Helleri'	Japanese holly
Taxus canadensis	Canadian yew
Taxus × media 'Densiformis'	Intermediate yew
Taxus × media 'Hatfieldii'	Hatfield yew
Taxus × media 'Hicksii'	Hicks yew

TREES

Large Trees

Acer rubrum	Red maple
Pinus Strobus	White pine
Quercus rubra	Red oak
Tsuga canadensis	Canadian hemlock

Small Trees and Tall Shrubs (bear fruit in summer; good for keeping wildlife away from crops)

Amelanchier canadensis	Shadbush, juneberry, or serviceberry
Cornus florida	Flowering dogwood

Small Deciduous Trees

Oxydendrum arboreum	Sorrel tree or sourwood

Small Trees and Tall Shrubs (holding fruit into winter)

Ilex verticillata	Winterberry
Viburnum dentatum	Arrowwood
Viburnum trilobum	Cranberry bush

Plants for Special Needs

TREES AND SHRUBS FOR SMALL SPACES

Deciduous Trees

Acer palmatum	Japanese maple
Amelanchier canadensis	Shadbush, juneberry, or serviceberry
Cercis canadensis	Redbud
Cornus florida	Flowering dogwood
Cornus kousa	Chinese dogwood
Cornus mas	Cornelian cherry dogwood
Magnolia stellata	Star magnolia
Oxydendrum arboreum	Sorrel tree or sourwood
Pyrus calleryana	Callery pear
Stewartia koreana	Korean stewartia

Deciduous Shrubs

Cotoneaster apiculatus	Cranberry cotoneaster
Euonymus alata 'Compacta'	Compact winged spindle tree
Forsythia viridissima 'Bronxensis'	Bronx forsythia
Fothergilla gardenii	Witch alder
Potentilla fruticosa	Shrubby cinquefoil
Rhododendron mucronulatum	Snow korean azalea
Spiraea japonica 'Alpina'	Japanese spiraea
Viburnum calesii 'Compactum'	Compact Korean viburnum
Viburnum Opulus 'Compactum'	Compact or dwarf cranberry bush viburnum

PLANTS FOR SHADE

Amelanchier canadensis	Shadbush, juneberry, or serviceberry
Aronia arbutifolia	Red chokeberry
Aronia melanocarpa	Black chokeberry
Cercis canadensis	Redbud
Clethra alnifolia	Summer-sweet
Cornus florida	Flowering dogwood
Hamamelis virginiana	Witch hazel
Kalmia latifolia	Mountain laurel
Leucothoe Fontanesiana	Drooping leucothoe
Lindera benzoin	Spicebush

Rhododendron calendulaceum,	Native azaleas
R. nudiflorum,	
R. viscosum	
Rhododendron carolinianum,	Native rhododendrons
R. maximum	
Symphoricarpos × Chenaultii	Snowberry
Symphoricarpos orbiculatus	Coralberry or Indian currant
Taxus canadensis	Canadian yew
Thuja occidentalis	American arborvitae
Tsuga canadensis	Canadian hemlock

PLANTS FOR FRAGRANCE

Clethra alnifolia	Summer-sweet
Comptonia peregrina	Sweet fern
Hamamelis mollis	Chinese witch hazel
Hamamelis virginiana	Common witch hazel
Magnolia spp.	Magnolia
Myrica pensylvanica	Bayberry
Rhododendron roseum	Rose-shell azalea
Rhododendron viscosum	Swamp azalea
Rhododendron spp.	Azalea and rhododendron hybrids
Viburnum carlesii	Korean viburnum
Wisteria floribunda	Japanese wisteria

PLANTS WITH UNIQUE BARK

Gray-Barked Trees and Shrubs

Acer rubrum	Red maple
Amelanchier canadensis	Shadbush, juneberry, or serviceberry
Clethra alnifolia	Summer-sweet
Cornus racemosa	Panicled dogwood
Viburnum Opulus	European cranberry bush
Viburnum trilobum	Highbush cranberry

Green-Barked Trees and Shrubs

| *Forsythia viridissima 'Bronxensis'* | Bronx forsythia |
| *Kerria japonica* | Japanese rose |

Yellow-Barked Trees and Shrubs

| *Cornus sericea 'Flaviramea'* | Golden-twig dogwood |

Red-Barked Trees and Shrubs

Acer griseum	Paperbark maple
Acer palmatum	Japanese maple
Cornus alba 'Sibirica'	Siberian dogwood
Cornus sericea	Red-osier dogwood
Stewartia pseudocamellia	Japanese stewartia
Viburnum Opulus 'Nanum'	Dwarf European cranberry bush

Smooth Barks (Silky or Velvety)

| *Amelanchier canadensis* | Shadbush, juneberry, or serviceberry |
| *Amelanchier laevis* | Serviceberry |

PLANTS WITH INTERESTING AUTUMN FOLIAGE

Small Trees

Acer palmatum	Japanese maple
Amelanchier canadensis	Shadbush, juneberry, or serviceberry
Amelanchier laevis	Allegheny serviceberry
Cercis canadensis	Redbud
Cornus florida	Flowering dogwood
Cornus kousa	Chinese dogwood
Cornus mas	Cornelian cherry dogwood
Magnolia stellata	Star magnolia

Medium to Large Trees

| *Acer platanoides* | Norway maple |
| *Tilia cordata* | Small-leaved European linden |

Shrubs

| *Clethra alnifolia* | Summer-sweet |
| *Hamamelis virginiana* | Witch hazel |

FURTHER READING

American National Standard for Aboveground/Onground Residential Swimming Pools. Alexandria, Va.: The National Spa and Pool Institute, 1991.

American National Standard of Public Swimming Pools. Alexandria, Va.: The National Spa and Pool Institute, 1991.

American Red Cross. *Lifeguarding.* Washington, D.C.: The American National Red Cross, 1990.

Ellis, Jeffrey L., and Carol Lee Fick. *National Pool and Waterpark Lifeguard Training.* Hoffman Estates, Ill.: National Recreation and Park Association, 1990.

Gabrielson, Alexander M. *Swimming Pools: A Guide to their Planning, Design and Operation,* 4th ed. Champaign, Ill.: Human Kinetics Publishers, Inc., 1987.

Johnson, Ralph L. *YMCA Pool Operations Manual.* Champaign, Ill.: Human Kinetics Publishers, Inc., 1989.

Kowalsky, Lester, ed. *Pool/Spa Operators Handbook.* San Antonio: National Swimming Pool Foundation, 1991.

Mitchell, Kirk P. *The Proper Management of Pool and Spa Water.* Decatur, Ga.: BioLab, Inc., 1988.

Murphy, Majorie M., and D.I. Forsten. *On the Guard: The YMCA Lifeguard Manual.* Champaign, Ill.: Human Kinetics Publishers, Inc., 1986.

Pool and Spa Market Study for the Year 1991. Alexandria, Va.: The National Spa and Pool Institute, 1992.

Pool and Spa News. Los Angeles: Leisure Publications.

Pool and Spa Water Chemistry: Testing and Treatment Guide with Tables. Sparks, Md.: Taylor Technologies, Inc.

The Pool Book. Decatur, Ga.: Bio-Lab, Inc.

Poolfax. Bradley, Ill.: Stranco, 1981.

Pope, James R., Ed.D. *A Manual on Sanitation, Filtration, and Disinfection.* Hoffman Estates, Ill.: National Recreation and Park Association.

Public Swimming Management II: A Manual on Safety, Training, Personnel and Programs. Hoffman Estates, Ill.: National Recreation and Park Association.

The Sensible Way to Enjoy Your Pool. Alexandria, Va.: The National Spa and Pool Institute, 1983.

Service Industry News. Torrance, Calif.: Service Industry Publications.

Standard for Residential Swimming Pools. Alexandria, Va.: The National Spa and Pool Institute, 1987.

Swimming and Diving. St. Louis: Mosby-Year Book, Inc.

Taylor, Charlie. *Everything You Always Wanted to Know About Pool Care.* Chino, Calif.: Service Industry Publications, 1989.

Torney, John A., and Robert D. Clayton. *Aquatic Instruction, Coaching and Management.* Minneapolis, Minn.: Burgess Publishing Company, 1970.

Water Book for Pool Professionals. Stamford, Conn.: Olin Corporation, 1984.

Water Quality and Treatment, 3rd ed. The American Water Works Association, Inc., 1971.

Williams, Kent G. *The Aquatic Facility Operator Manual.* Hoffman Estates, Ill.: National Recreation and Park Association, National Aquatic Section, 1991.

TRADE PUBLICATIONS

United States

Aqua
Athletic Business Publications
1846 Hoffman Street
Madison, WI 53704

Aquatics International
Communications Channels
6151 Powers Ferry Road N.W.
Atlanta, GA 30339-2941

Parks and Recreation
2775 South Quincy Street
Arlington, VA 22206

Pool and Spa News
Leisure Publications
3923 West 6th Street
Los Angeles, CA 90020

Service Industry News
Service Industry Publications
P.O. Box 2909
Torrance, CA 90509-2909

Canada
Pool and Spa Marketing
Hubbard Marketing
270 Esna Park Drive
Unit 12
Markham, Ontario
L3R 1H3
Canada

Australia
Pool and Spa Review
Leisure Publications
4 Coppabella Road
P.O. Box 81
Dural, N.S.W. 2158
Australia

France
Ambiance Piscines
18, rue d'Alsace-Lorraine
78530 Buc
France

Germany
Schwimmbad & Sauna
Höhenstrasse 17
Postfach 1329
D-7012 Fellbach
Germany

Italy
Piscine Oggi
Via G. Amendola, 11
I-40121 Bologna
Italy

Spain
Piscinas XXI
Av. Parallel 180
E-08015 Barcelona
Spain

United Kingdom
Swimming Pool News
172 London Road
GB-Guilford, Surrey
GU1 1XR
United Kingdom

PHOTOGRAPHY CREDITS

Courtesy of American Chem-Tech, Inc., Phoenix, Arizona: pp. 84, 85
Courtesy of Aquatic Pools, Sherman Oaks, California: pp. 41 bottom, 76, 98, 99, 104, 105
Illustrations by Steven Arcella: pp. 78 all, 113
© Joe Barnell/Superstock: p. 50
Courtesy of Bomanite, Madera, California: pp. 90, 91; Homeowners: Tom and Lee Lockwood of Connecticut Bomanite Systems
Courtesy of California Pools, San Diego, California: p. 102
© Ron Chapple/FPG International: p. 73 top
© Color Box/FPG International: p. 49
Courtesy of Cover Pools, Inc., Salt Lake City, Utah: p. 128
© Grey Crawford: p. 129
© Ron Dahlquist/Superstock: pp. 14-15
Courtesy of Dolphin Pools, Dallas, Texas: p. 80 left
© Max Eckert/FPG International: pp. 21, 27, 30, 56 bottom, 124
© Phillip H. Ennis: pp. 45 top, 46, 48, 56 top, 64, 66, 68, 119
© Feliciano: pp. 7, 135
© Gerald French/FPG International: pp. 24-25, 44, 110
© Mark E. Gibson: pp. 11, 118
Courtesy of Gym and Swim, Louisville, Kentucky: pp. 94, 95
© Steve Joester/FPG International: p. 127
© Bruce Katz: p. 45 bottom
© Dennis Krukowski: p. 75
© Jenifer Levy: p. 53; Design: Mojo Stumer Architects
© E. Alan McGee/FPG International: pp. 1, 22, 42
© Fred McKinney/FPG International: p. 120
© Richard Mendelkorn: pp. 3, 26; Pool architecture-Lindsay Associates, Landscape design-Mr. Ralph Hartman, Pool Constuction-Mr. Ted Richards; 18
Courtesy of Modern Pool and Spa, Inc., Columbus, Mississippi: pp. 80 right, 81, 82, 83, 96, 97
Courtesy of Mutual Pools and Staff, Campsie, New South Wales, Australia; Photography by Roger Hanlon: pp. 100, 101
© Photo Nimatallah/Art Resource: p. 9 top
Courtesy of Paco Pools, Baldwin, New York: pp. 12, 13 top, 20, 89
© Maria Pape/FPG International: p. 108
© Robert Perron: pp. 19, 58 top, 115
© Robert Reif/FPG International: p. 58 bottom
© John Rigo, California Pools and Spas, San José, California: pp. 33, 35, 36, 37, 71, 106, 107
Courtesy of Rizzo Pools, Hartford, Connecticut: pp. 62, 87, 92, 93, 131
© Eric Roth: p. 111
© Bill Rothschild: p. 16, 43
© Schuster/Superstock: p. 132
Courtesy of Solar Pool Enclosures of New York, Holbrook, New York: p. 73 bottom
Courtesy of St. Louis Tub and Spa, Kirkwood, Missouri: p. 72
© Tim Street-Porter: pp. 2, 29, 39, 41 top, 51, 54, 57 top, 63, 123; 13 bottom, 61: Architect: David Connors; 28: Architect: John Woolf; 55: Designer: Hutton Wilkinson, Landscaping: Morgan Wheelock
© Jeffrey Sylvester/FPG International: p. 133
© Werner Forman Archive/Art Resource: p. 9 bottom

INDEX